Pilgrimage

STEPHEN MAY

Pilgrimage

A Journey
Through Colorado's History and Culture

ILLUSTRATED BY THE AUTHOR

Swallow Press/Ohio University Press
ATHENS OHIO/CHICAGO/LONDON

Library of Congress Cataloging-in-Publication Data

May, Stephen.
  Pilgrimage: a journey through Colorado's history and culture.

  1. Colorado—Description and travel—1981-   . 2. Colorado—History.
3. May, Stephen—Journeys—Colorado.   I. Title.
F781.3.M39   1986   978.8′033   86-5783
ISBN 0-8040-0882-5
ISBN 0-8040-0883-3 (pbk.)

Oh, do not ask, "What is it?"
Let us go and make our visit.
—Eliot

Contents

Acknowledgments

Chapter 3:   From *Uncle Dick Wootton*, by Howard Conard (Chicago: W. E. Dibble & Co., 1890).

Chapter 10: From *The Colorado*, by Frank Waters (New York: Rinehart & Co., 1946).

Chapter 13: From *A Lady's Life in the Rocky Mountains*, by Isabella Bird (New York: G. P. Putnam's Sons, 1881).

Chapter 14: From *Echoes from Arcadia*, by Francis C. Young, published anonymously (Denver: for private circulation, 1903).

Chapter 15: From *Specimen Days*, by Walt Whitman (New York: Literary Classics of the United States, 1982).

Chapter 16: From *Leaves of Grass*, by Walt Whitman (Philadelphia: D. McKay, 1900).

Preface

The idea for this book probably came to me in Cape Cod or London years or months ago, places and times a world away from where it was to be realized. I had simply become accustomed to living in Colorado, unconsciously enjoying its wildness and absorbing its Algerian sun and dry upland air.

But there are times that just when you understand someone he or she turns a different face toward you. And there came a growing suspicion that I did not understand much about the face of the Colorado I thought I knew.

This book is the fulfillment of that search. I was determined to seek out a soul, without even knowing if it indeed had one. But I sensed that it did. From that point my thirst led me to the road.

I have borrowed from the voices of the past. They are such excellent teachers, and I have tried to weave their views into my narrative. Besides, perhaps they knew something I did not. They saw a world I had no opportunity to see. And I discovered through their eyes that a new vision of Colorado became clear— so I am as deeply indebted to them as I am to the land and the people.

I am also indebted to the great English travel writers, who brushed with their words some truly glorious canvases of Sardinia, Britain, France, and Italy: Hilaire Belloc, D. H. Lawrence, and John Hillaby. Their visions put me there and made travel writing something more than just the discussion of the number of guest rooms in the historic country hotel down the lane. I could also mention H. V. Morton, who in the late twenties took his low-slung roadster through the backroads and byways in *In Search of England.* He gave new exposure to the remote villages and revealed some small places with large histories. John Steinbeck's *Travels with Charley* is a continuing source of inspiration.

The simple fact about looking for a soul is that you can't overlook anything to find it. You can't turn your nose up at famous resorts, for it just may be there you find it staring you in the face. You can't be a recluse either, holed up at the end of the earth, scratching in the soil to find that one grain which reveals the universe. You can't be sure of anything, so you must cover the field.

With this in mind, I planned my journey beforehand, intending on stopping here, hiking there, exploring this, and rediscovering that. There were constant surprises as with any decent adventure. There were places and people that made me swell with admiration; there were others that turned the heart to chalk. Some towns I could not wait to be rid of, and others seduced me with their history and unique beauty. But through it all the mission of my pilgrimage never left me. I wanted something. And it was something more than lectures and guidebooks could give me. So, like Siddhartha, I made a journey to find out what it was all about. And like all meaningful journeys, I discovered as much about myself as I did about the towns and country I traveled through.

I began in late summer and finished in time for the first of the heavy snows to fall in the mountains. I carried maps, a camera, notebooks, sketchbooks, and a volume of Whitman. If Whitman stands out in the weave of the narrative like a bright and gritty thread, it is perhaps a reflection of his enduring spirit and the Colorado he loved.

In addition to these essential items, I also hauled around the usual paraphernalia, half of which I never saw. The experienced traveler knows what to leave behind, but as there are more beasts of burden than racehorses on the road, I assume that most people, like me, have not yet learned from their mistakes.

My objective for this book was to have the reader come with me and experience what I experienced. I wanted her or him in the front seat, hearing, feeling, and seeing the same things I was.

Too many travel writers had left me, the reader, at home while they went out and had all the fun. I also wanted to tie Colorado to the rest of the world—physically, culturally, historically—and present it as part of one complete fabric. As I will alert the reader in the following pages, we are not isolated, but share an important heritage with Europe, Asia, Africa, the Americas, and perhaps, the universe.

My idea was not to try to cover the region entirely, but to randomly select the places I thought might yield what I was looking for. If I have omitted your favorite town, forest, scenic attraction, or personality, then I shall only feel ashamed if in the end I have not beguiled you with mine.

S.M.
Colorado Springs

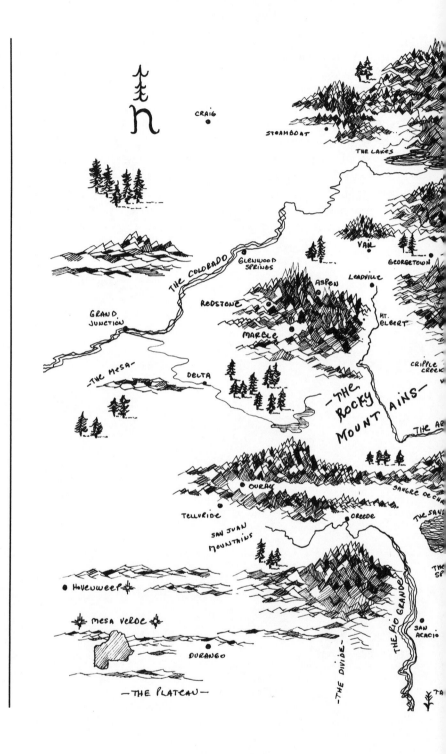

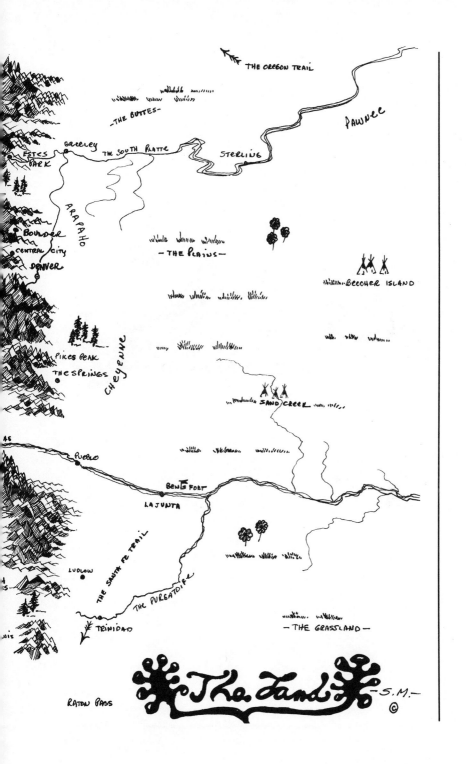

1

The Enduring Peak

'LITTLE LONDON'
September 20:

Narratives that begin in beautiful weather are always suspect. I sense that the writer has dreamed up a gem of a day at the expense of the unsuspecting reader. Great adventures are born in cold wet dawns with no hope of sun—and this beginning was to be no exception.

When you begin the journey of a lifetime, you expect all the elements to submit to even the feeblest of wishes. But they simply would not obey. It rained and the morning howled its way into being. It remained miserably wet and cold just before my departure, although the wind showed signs of slackening. Even the names of places that burn like soft stars in the back of the mind—the Chilkoot Pass, the Appian Way, the Nile, places that keep us from our jobs and condemn us to the road—failed to inspire me, and their romantic names seemed more like cruel sirens singing in the dark morning air.

But the rotten weather turned out not to be an omen, for at about eight-thirty the sky cleared and revealed, scoured and new, the dark blue ridge of the Front Range, which separates one half of Colorado from the other. Around nine I stood at a point, where in September 1879, Walt Whitman rumbled through Colorado Springs on the Denver and Rio Grande Railroad. Peering out the west window, his delicate brows arched, he remarked that Pikes Peak made him a "little disappointed" and that he "had expected something stunning."

I imagine that after Whitman had experienced the awesome drop at Kenosha Pass the previous week Pikes Peak looked painfully redundant. Among the Disneyland of vistas that he encountered on his Colorado trip that year, Pikes Peak was a sadly neglected attraction.

But I still find it imposing—rising, when backlit, like Khufu's pyramid and dominating the city and ridges below. It has the presence of a god. It commands the valley with speechless authority, and its clouds and mists indicate how sunny and rainless an afternoon you're likely to have. It also, of course, defines the direction for hundreds of miles around. Once, though, a middle-aged tourist hurried up to a policeman on a Colorado Springs' street and announced boldly:

"Mister, I'm lost."

The officer dryly responded: "Lady, there's the Peak. What does that tell you?"

Confused, she finally blurted out: "It tells me that there is a big mountain behind that big building, and very little else." And then she stomped off, obviously embarrassed.

Even when coming to Colorado, it is encouraged that you assign a direction, beforehand, to important and unmistakable landmarks.

Choosing the sight of Whitman's remark about the Pikes Peak to begin my journey was more symbolic than obligatory. Perhaps I wanted to reassure myself of its splendor and its power. Now the clamor of the Burlington Northerns at Garden of the Gods Road drowns out the creakings and fidgetings of Whitman's wooden carriage. Cars and service trucks rumble down the road past the platoons of electronic and computer firms.

From this point south is Colorado Springs, William Palmer's enterprising city, and the Broadmoor, Spencer Penrose's mirror image of the enchanting Italian Renaissance villas. North is the Air Force Academy with its pronged chapel. East is Pulpit Rock and beyond that the suburban spread-eagle pins one hand of Colorado Springs to the plains. The grasslands flow eastward, undulating over creeks and arid gulleys, threading pine forests and farmlands until they reach Kansas. To the west is the Front

Range, Pike's Peak, and beyond are the high snowy ramparts of the Continental Divide.

Whitman headed south in 1879, struck east at Pueblo, and eventually returned to his home in Camden, New Jersey. All the way he lionized the prairies, the mountains, the skies—symbols of freedom that ultimately made him feel uncomfortable and vulnerable. And I, another pilgrim seeking a different shrine, climbed into the Jeep and headed west.

What impressed Whitman, and others who streamed into the West, is the space—horizontal space. Unbroken by trees, the landscape stretches and dips into an infinity of distant pine and wheat brown grasses. Here is the space you need for big thoughts and dreams, for reflection and action, and here is the limitless edge for new ideas to drift with impunity.

But the wind violates the openness. There are breezes in Java and gentle trades in the Pacific, but there are fierce winds in this part of Colorado. From January through April they roar down from the north, sometimes cold, sometimes lukewarm. The plains and foothills rest under ribbons of fresh snow; the sun appears meekly and all is silent but the wind. Persistent and alive, it shoves its fist down over the hogbacks and open grass-lands. It relents sometimes only in the late night, when its last murmurings accompany dreams.

When the violent winds drop, the true chinook is born. It is the warmest and softest of north winds. Sometimes in February a good chinook can raise temperatures into the sixties. Then there is the driest warmth in the wind, and the most delicious coolness on its traces. Particularly here, where the mountains meet the plains, the weather acts like a revolving door—alternately, without warning, it opens and closes, admitting crashing thunder-storms on the heels of balmy morning breezes. It confounds tourists as well as denizens. The most arid savanna north of Colorado Springs can change into a river from a passing shower.

In September, though, the colors are hard and bright. The low sun causes the blue gray shadows of the peaks to lengthen and deepen in color. The bald pink summits declare themselves against the cobalt sky. The great monoliths in the Garden of the Gods, rising in thick and sometimes paper-thin diagonals, are of the purest red. In late September the scarlets become startlingly vivid against the arid sky, as the huge ancient stones defy the seasons, people, and elements of another year.

Here on any day in spring, summer, or fall, climbers scramble up these awesome rocks. The most dangerous visitors come empty-handed. Wives, children, men with sodas in their hands, absentmindedly ascend a rock and gape down helplessly. They end up being assisted down by park rangers, or too often, are carried out unconscious by helicopter rescue squads. Others, who respect the power of these stones, come prepared with ropes and climbing gear and experience. But most of the tourists have left now; the climbers disperse over the Garden and challenge the mammoth red slopes.

The drop is sheer. Up through the shadows the climbers in twos and threes finger their way. The ropes dangle in long commas; still they grope upward. But unlike Sisyphus they control the rock by toiling *around* it. I used to wonder what drove these proud few to spend their entire day rubbing their noses on a rock. I think I know, now. A student from Sweden explained:

"There is nothing like this in my country—nothing like *this.* It's so big. You want to be part of it."

Words sometimes are such feeble creatures, but I sensed what he was trying to communicate. I left him there in a swarm of climbers, knowing that to wrap one's body around that vastness was something akin to floating among the stars.

I passed Manitou Springs, surely one of the most Victorian hillsides outside Britain. It has the bubbling creeks which gave its neighboring city to the east, Colorado Springs, the other half of its name. Just above the city, before you emerge into Ute Pass, you can look back at the entire stage of westward expansion. There is Kansas—way out there, over the pine and oak and cornfields, out and beyond and further yet, east toward the Mississippi, where settlers gathered their wagons and dreams around St. Louis. Then their trails, the Santa Fe, the Mormon, the Oregon, spread like fingers out into the West, took them to the Rockies and the Pacific.

I drove just north of Pikes Peak, named after Zebulon Pike, who, in late November 1806, abandoned all attempts to climb it. If Whitman didn't think it was formidable, Pike certainly did. On November 27, Pike and his climbing party braved the waist-deep

snow and below-zero temperatures in an assault on the summit.
After struggling for fifteen miles, Pike observed that another six-
teen miles of near vertical ascent lay ahead of them. Pike ran out
of daylight and warm temperatures, and having "only light over-
alls on and no stockings," decided to terminate the expedition.

It was probably the most prudent decision of a most prudent
man. Even in summer, experienced climbers on Pikes Peak are
aware of the dangers of hypothermia. In Pike's case, dropping
temperatures and insufficient clothing would have insured
death, possibly shortly thereafter.

But Pike, having failed to climb the peak that bears his name,
didn't sound like a beaten man. Consider the entry in his diary
for the next day, November 28:

"Marched at nine o'clock. Kept straight down the creek to
avoid the hills. At half past one o'clock shot two buffaloes, when
we made the first full meal we had eaten for three days. En-
camped in a valley under a shelving rock. The land here was very
rich, and covered with old Ietan camps." Is there anything but
business and the delight in obtaining a meal in this entry? There
is nothing to suggest that the magnificent summit commanding
the valley, the Garden, the distant plains, and glistening ridges
had in any way made him a bitter man.

As I continued driving, the mountains huddling around me, I
reached over the gears and switched off the radio. It is one of the
great prerogatives of civilization and one of the conscious acts of
rebellion left to us. Everyone talks about turning on the radio
and television, but the true joy is in the reverse procedure. Besides, the birds were out, the dark green pines sprang from their
coarse salmon sands, the creeks splashed past me, and I was
bound for the heart of America—not the geographical heart, but
the great mythical one. I was headed for the sources of the Rio
Grande, the Colorado, the Arkansas, the Platte, which like arter-
ies and veins flee the central mountains and feed Kansas, the
backside of California, and the vast dry rib cage of New Mexico
and Texas.

All the sounds of a great muscle beating were around me.
Could Mozart, Stevie Wonder, or a radio psychologist make it any
more enticing?

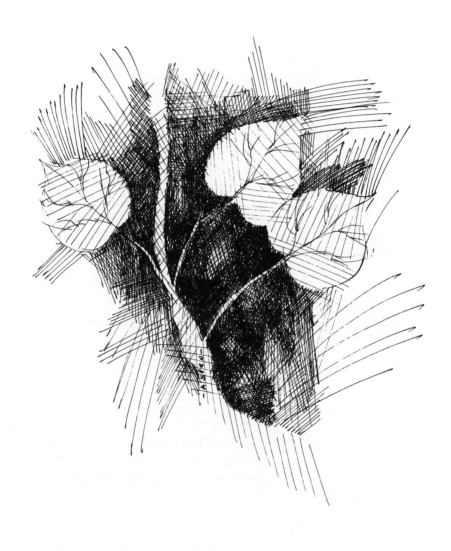

2

Mammon

After circling the backbone of Pikes Peak, the road drops from the trees in a sweeping arc into Cripple Creek. With the Sangre de Christos a purple backdrop, Cripple Creek sits in a vulnerable cavern, its pockmarked and sulphorous hills open to the southern sun.

There are towns where the ghosts are real, the sound of spurs not imagined, and the rustlings of horses and harnesses are as near as the beating of the heart. This is such a place. Bennett Avenue looks eminently respectable. Clustered around it, the houses are efficient and utilitarian structures meant only for hanging your hat. In all, the town modestly wears its rowdy western reputation amid a flourishing tourist trade.

But in the last decades of the nineteenth century respectability wore thin. Into these streets was jammed the whole lot of humanity: assayers, newspapermen, fortune hunters, outfitters, saloon keepers, itinerants. They came from the ends of the earth; feverishly they clamored their way over the plains and then down into these valleys. They set up camps, worked the mines, and fought the fights of desperate people—right out here under the blazing sun of Cripple Creek and Victor. Then one day some of them left, and others followed. The gold stayed in the earth, but the men and women moved on to California, the Klondike, to other gold pickings and other fast times. Some limped home, back East, their only wares a few nuggets of copper pyrite.

But in its heyday, Cripple Creek looked like Baghdad. And down Bennett Avenue, surrounded by the din, a young Lowell Thomas sold newspapers. Only a wisp of a boy in a Stetson, Thomas nevertheless began to show early the self-assurance that followed him all his life as a journalist and adventurer. And perhaps no other journalist of the twentieth century has had the temerity to shuffle and redeal all the cards handed him by God, Fate, and Victor, Colorado.

He was born in Ohio, but his father, a doctor (and reclusive scholar), moved the family to Colorado and settled in Victor in 1900. Thomas was shaped by the rough-and-tumble life of the camps.

In Victor, Cripple Creek's timid twin, a certain rawness and neglect still persist. Surveying the town from the porch of Thomas's home, you can see the Gothic church and the garish yellow mountains, prospected then abandoned, that loom like angry landlords over the quiet tenants below.

But Thomas wanted more than the action of Victor and Cripple Creek could offer him. He combined an education at Northern Indiana University (earning two degrees) with a love for the dramatic and unique that, I sense, he absorbed from the teeming streets of Cripple Creek.

By late 1917 he was in Cairo, Egypt, lured by the dearth of journalists covering the Middle East campaign. While war raged in Europe, Thomas and cameraman Harry Chase pursued the British and Allenby's efforts to wrest Jerusalem from the Turks. And it was in Jerusalem, shortly after its capture by the British, that Thomas saw in a swirl of Arab faces the blue-eyed bedouin, T. E. Lawrence.

Now some are beaten into fortune, and some have fortune thrown upon them. I have a suspicion that the first exchange of glances between Lawrence and Thomas qualifies as the latter, and was one of those superb strokes of luck somehow reserved for other people. The encounter of the two shortly thereafter, however, was something like the meeting of air and fire: the enigmatic, mystical Lawrence and the pragmatic, hard-nosed Thomas. But Thomas was convinced that he had discovered the great story of the war—a young Briton who single-handedly had

organized the disparate Arab tribes and shaped them into a formidable fighting unit. It was Lawrence's personality, though, that
fascinated Thomas. Here was the warrior-scholar, the poet-
activist, the child-man, the perfect equilibrium of opposites that
you find more in the abstract than in truth.

After the war Thomas showcased Lawrence's exploits by taking a rather shallow and contrived stage show on a world tour. It
was an enormous financial success. Thomas went on to become
a renowned journalist both in America and abroad. Lawrence,
elusive to the end, took an assumed name and disappeared from
world attention. He burrowed deep into the woods of Dorset
and remained there until his death in 1935, far from Thomas and
a world away from the sands of Arabia.

During the boisterous years, from 1900 to 1918, Victor-Cripple
Creek was host to the best and worst of the itinerant boxers. They
worked as bouncers in saloons, or like Jack Dempsey toiled as
muckers in the mines.

Dempsey was born in Manassa, Colorado, just a short ride
north of the New Mexico border. He fought his way through the
mining camps of Colorado and Utah, picking scraps with amateurs and cheap thugs. Here under this blistering sun, boxers
tangled in crude, makeshift rings for fifty-dollar purses. There
was Dempsey, a raw kid who had the energy of the camps in him,
a shirtless, animal vitality, that when turned loose could be sold
as entertainment to hordes of roaring miners. He had an up-
from-the-legs strength that swelled up through his abdomen and
chest, culminating in a face that was uneven and struck with me-
nace. And he could take heat: not this Sahara up here in Victor,
but the hot, thick, wet stuff of Memphis, Philadelphia, and
Atlanta.

Then he got good, the hook connected with increasing fre-
quency, and he left the squalor of the camps. He went to Salt Lake
City, Oakland, and San Francisco. In 1919 he beat Jess Willard in
Toledo, Ohio, for the heavyweight title.

"Dempsey told me Jess had been drinkin'."

The old man with the raisin face suddenly grew still. He
looked out over the hills of Victor and the bright houses.

"Think Dempsey was right. Jess hit the canvas like a ton of
bricks. The 'Mauler' was some fighter. Fought here as an ama-

teur. Steel fists, springs in his legs. Packed a real wallop. Jack's trainer used to lie about his weight, ya know. The Willard fight—they jacked it up from 180 to 184. Willard weighed about 250. Guess they wanted a decent match for the crowd.

"Hell, that was fightin' then—real life to it. A young kid then was boxin' every month, sometimes every other week. Now it's every year, when they do fight. So damned disgustin'—a man can't fight a good fight anymore."

Right across the street where Jack Dempsey punched some unlucky misfit in the nose, I found a store whose insides looked more like a warehouse. The sign said Antiques, but I knew better upon entering.

Every bit of flotsam and jetsam that had been dragged West, from the courts of Russia, garages in Pennsylvania, and barns in Virginia, was deposited on dusty vanities or dangled from the raftered cathedral ceiling. Couches, chairs, tables, splintered bed posts and bric-a-brac were squeezed into tight rows with only a few feet to walk between them. The air smelled of galoshes and wood and the New Deal.

The funny thing about it was that I enjoyed it at first. In the middle of Victor I was also smack-dab in the center of the world. I pulled out drawers with sparkling broaches in them from the Jazz Age, or in the next motion I scrutinized a harness from nineteenth-century Germany.

All the time that I moved slowly toward the rear of the store, I noticed that I was dodging the proprietor. He went down one packed aisle, I scurried down the other. I hid in a wilderness of brass lamps, absentmindedly fingering a tin of "Sultan's Choice." Then I knew what secret fear was bothering me. The man would ask: "May I help you?" Yes, he would spring that on me, and that would mean that he *knew* where everything was in this vast barn. He knew every shoe nail and hairbrush and where they came from and when. I shuffled around and he followed. I was almost to the back of the store when he caught me by the Mexican blankets.

"May I help you?"

He said it. He knew. He could have worked at the United Nations or the Library of Congress. The White House! But, no, he worked across the street from where Dempsey used to punish upstarts. He was planted in Victor, Colorado, to astound tourists.

I shook my head, smiled, and muttered a few words of thanks. He nodded and turned to arrange a cluster of coins on a nearby table. I returned to the "Sultan's Choice." But my heart wasn't in it.

I slowly edged toward the front door, took one long last look at the vastness of the shop, saw the man who knew too much disappear among his things, then headed straight for the Jeep. I pulled out into the sun and dust of Victor with a renewed respect for small towns.

I am a fair person. I walk among the streets of white cities, smile at children, follow donkeys up among dry olive trees, and leave American dollars where I go. I only smuggle one sugar packet from restaurants.

But the countryside around Victor and the banks of Clear Creek east of Black Hawk test my judiciousness. Mining equipment, some of it suffering from decades of rust, lies like the dry, discarded chicken bones of an afternoon picnic. Conveyor belts rise like tarnished javelins to the sun. Black-eyed Susans poke through useless tires by the roadside.

I know that in these bones and javelins resides a mining town's desperate beauty. I also know that they would be better off in a museum or junkyard. As it is, their memories stay with me on afternoon rides, and reach across weeks to shake me from the moment a flower opens or dies.

3

Pueblo

THE ARKANSAS RIVER
September 21:

The especially fine weather held through the morning and would hold for the next few days. Bursts of yellow lined the road as it twisted out of the mountains. I headed east for a brief stop at Pueblo and picked up the gushing of the Arkansas River on my right.

The Arkansas begins in the mountains north of Leadville, turns south through the central basin, and below Salida begins its inexorable flow eastward and southward through Kansas, Oklahoma, until it finally joins the Mississippi above Arkansas City. The Arkansas River connects Pueblo to Rocky Ford to Wichita to Tulsa and Fort Smith; the silt that accompanies it joins Colorado to Arkansas and the Mississippi delta, and to the Gulf of Mexico and the world.

Francis Parkman and Richard Henry Dana were both from Boston. Parkman's book *The Oregon Trail* and Dana's *Two Years before the Mast* are two of the best American travel books of the nineteenth century. Dana's story sketches the routine of a common seaman on a voyage from Boston to California; Parkman's classic records his vivid impressions of the eastern reaches of the trail West in 1846.

It is noteworthy that the two great statements in American travel were written within a decade of each other. Both are by inexperienced writers who managed to articulate their experiences with candor and insight.

As a boy growing up in California, I remember tracing the route of Dana's journey up the coast. Standing on the bluffs of Palos Verdes and San Pedro, I would mark where he came ashore and determine roughly where the brig *Pilgrim* could be moored safely. From there the vast sea looked eternal but unknowable, stretching into an infinity of glitter.

As I stand now, looking over the plains and Pueblo, I can visualize the arrival of Parkman in late August 1846, and feel with certainty the connection of Boston to California, of nature to man, this prairie grass to the enduring river winding to the sea. To travel is to create entire networks of places, people, griefs, joys, and rejections, firing off like muffled explosions in the mind. And like the river and the sea, the mind is an endless estuary of ebbing and flowing associations.

The city of Pueblo in 1846 was nothing more than what Parkman called "a rude trading fort . . . surrounded by a wall of mud, miserably cracked and dilapidated." In early August he had left Fort Laramie with a group of men and a Paiute squaw bound for Pueblo and Bent's Fort. Throughout the middle of August, Parkman followed the ravines and creeks that flowed south into the Arkansas River. He passed in succession Cherry Creek, east of Denver, Black Forest, and then finally found Fountain Creek which surges toward Pueblo.

Parkman was somehow the perfect foil to the ruggedness of the land. He maintained a strict Eastern demeanor and was rather a sober judge of the customs of southern Colorado. Above all, he disliked people who didn't mind their own business. Once near the Arkansas River, Parkman's party encountered an oncoming wagon whose driver yelled:

"Whar are ye from, Californy?"

Parkman: "No."

"Santy Fee?"

"No—the mountains."

"What yer been doing thar? Tradin'?"

Parkman: "No."

"Trappin'?"

"No."

"Huntin'?"

"No."

"Emigratin'?"

"No."

"What *have* you been doing, God damn ye?"

By this time, as Parkman relates, the driver was screaming the question as the wagons pulled farther and farther apart. Even days and months of isolation could not shake one scruple from its firm lodging in tradition.

There is no way around it. Pueblo is not an inspiring city, nor will it ever challenge the beauty of Santa Fe. But it is certain that Pueblo has one of the richest histories of any city near the Front Range.

I drove downtown, parked the Jeep, and prepared a reconnaissance of the city by foot.

In Europe you learn quickly that cities devour motorists and the faster you can walk away from the car the better. Even in Pueblo, where the traffic is neither hellish nor modest, you are forced onto your feet.

I promptly found that Pueblo is a city of memorials—they sprout like the over 2,000 varieties of wild flowers surrounding the city. Just south of City Hall, I walked up to the granite monument marking the site of Fort Pueblo. It bears the inscription: "Old Fort Pueblo was on the Arkansas River, site of the Indian Massacre in 1854 . . . "

I suppose that I looked puzzled enough because a remarkable lady in her seventies stopped next to me. There are gurus who reveal the infinite and there are retired librarians who know a lot about everything. I was in luck, and she was not the former.

We sat down on a bench nearby, and she explained that the site of the historic fort was just north of the river. It was now a parking lot.

The ironies of history have a way of becoming apparent in the technology of the present. I wondered what Francis Parkman would think about the fate of Fort Pueblo, and if he could imagine rows of dusty Subarus and Fords parked under its walls.

And what about the massacre? I asked.

It seems that on Christmas day, 1854, the inhabitants of the fort had been cautioned not to let in the Ute Indians, who had been acting suspiciously. But it *was* Christmas. The seventeen inhabitants got roaring drunk and admitted the Indians for a little celebration. Things got out of hand. The Utes turned on the people of the fort, killing all except a young girl, two children, and a man called Romaldo. He struggled outside, a bullet hole in his tongue, and described the gruesome annhilation to his rescuers in sign language.

After that incident, mountain men and traders no longer held their rendezvous at the fort, and Pueblo lost much of its support as the economic base for the upper Arkansas River.

What about the mountain men? Were they as resourceful as we're led to believe?

"Uncle Dick" Wootton was. He was the shrewdest businessman west of the Mississippi. Once he drove 9,000 sheep from New Mexico to California and hardly lost an animal. He came to Pueblo in 1853 to capitalize on the trade centered in the city. He used to swap fresh livestock for footsore ones from the East. The latter would be rested and cared for until they could be swapped again for more disabled cattle and oxen. His herds trebled and so did his profits.

He later opened a saloon in Denver—but he wasn't a merchant at heart, so he returned to southern Colorado. He helped build a road over Raton Pass into New Mexico and collected tolls at the point of a gun. I suppose that groups entering Colorado had to pay their dues, but it is difficult to visualize Dick the recipient of tokens thrown by soiled and speeding pedestrians.

The Mountain Man's Tale

I had long had in mind the building of a stage road through the Raton Pass . . . I had been over the mountains so often, had in fact lived in them so many years, that I knew almost every available pass in Colorado and New Mexico, and understood just about how the travel ran in various directions. I knew that the Raton Pass was a natural highway connecting settlements already in existence, and destined to be a thoroughfare for other settlements which would spring up in south eastern Colorado and northeastern New Mexico. Barlow

and Sanderson, the proprietors of the Santa Fe stage line, were
anxious to change their route so as to pass through Trinidad . . . and the freighters generally wanted to come
through that way. How to get through the pass was the problem, however, for all of them.

A trail led through the canyon it is true, but that was almost
impassable for anything but saddle horses and pack animals at
any time and entirely impassable for wagon trains or stages in
the winter time. Nobody knew this better than I did, because I
had come through the pass on my way to Denver in 1858 and
spent nearly a month traveling a distance of fifty miles with a
comparatively light wagon load. What I proposed to do was to
go into this winding, rock-ribbed mountain pass and hew out
a road which, barring grades, should be as good as the average turnpike. I expected to keep this road in good repair and
charge toll for traveling over it, and thought I could see a
good business ahead of me.

Only the Indians were exempted from paying the fixed
rates . . . I did make one exception . . . in favor of officers
and parties who were in pursuit of horse and cattle thieves.
Stealing cattle and horses in Colorado and running them into
New Mexico got to be quite a business, and the same band of
thieves that drove Colorado stock into New Mexico would re-
cross the line with stock stolen from the Mexicans. . . .
Gangs used to pass through here frequently.

One morning, I remember, just as I was starting out to work
I met a young fellow riding a fine-looking horse without
either saddle or bridle. I suspected it was stolen, but was not
sure of it until half an hour later when a pursuing party came
along and gave the information. Learning that the man they
were looking for was not far ahead, they galloped along, and
in the afternoon of the same day they came back, bringing
with them the stolen horse. I asked them if they had captured
the thief and they said, "Yes, we captured him, and if anybody
inquires for him, you can tell them that they can find his remains over in New Mexico, where his career as a horsethief
ended." . . .

One of the most daring and successful daylight stage rob-
beries that I remember was perpetrated by two men when the
east-bound stage was coming up on the south side of the

Raton Mountains one day about ten o'clock in the forenoon.
. . . There were four passengers in the coach, all men, but
their hands went up at the same instant that the driver
dropped his reins, and struck an attitude that suited the
robbers. Then, while one of the men stood guard, the other
stepped up to the stage and ordered the treasure box thrown
off. This demand was complied with and the box was broken
open and rifled of its contents, which fortunately were not of
great value.

The passengers were compelled to hand out their watches
and other jewelry, as well as what money they had in their
pockets, and then the driver was directed to move on up the
road. In a minute after the robbery had been completed the
robbers had disappeared with their booty, and that was the
last seen of them by that particular coach load of passengers.
The men who planned and executed that robbery were two
cool, level-headed and daring scoundrels known as Chucka-
luck and Magpie. They were killed soon after this occurrence
by a member of their own band whose name was Steward. A
reward of a thousand dollars had been offered for their capture and this tempted Steward to kill them one night when
they were asleep in camp . . .

My toll road was a success financially from the time I completed it up to the time it was paralleled by the Santa Fe Railroad. Then I got out of the way of the locomotive and turned
my business over to the railroad company. I have but one ob-
jection to railroads, by the way, and that is they drive the game
out of the country. . . . Before the railroad was built I used
to sit on the front porch of my house and shoot deer, but
since that time I have had to get out and skirmish around a
good deal to find even a jack rabbit.

Dick Wootton's Pass (Raton Pass) is ninety miles due south of
Pueblo, the only avenue from Colorado's mineral-rich Front
Range to Santa Fe and Albuquerque.

The Santa Fe railroad snorted through the pass for the first
time in 1879, ending months of fierce competition with Gen.
William Palmer's Denver and Rio Grande for the rights of
passage.

Both companies held Pueblo. Both knew that Dick Wootton's

sinuous little toll road contained some of the most valued dirt in Colorado. Beyond it lay the sprawling, naked Southwest and its network of connections to the Pacific coast.

Both companies began a series of furtive moves to seize the land. In the summer of 1878 Palmer sent a large grading crew to Pueblo and instructed them to secure the pass. But W. B. Strong of the Santa Fe was one move ahead of Palmer. He organized his grading crew just below the pass. In the early morning hours of a summer day, the crew began clearing the snaking grade into New Mexico. It was pitch-dark and they worked by lamps. By four A.M., just before first light, the Santa Fe's survey party was far ahead of the grading crew and working their way to the summit. At daybreak the Santa Fe grading crew looked back to see Palmer's gang just beginning to work their way up the winding ascent. Four hours of construction time had given the pass to the Santa Fe railroad, and they went on grading and laying track through the pass and down into Santa Fe.

But afterward the steep ascent proved too exhausting for Santa Fe locomotives. A more robust locomotive was commissioned, later named the "Uncle Dick," in memory of the man who assessed tolls, punished rustlers, shot deer from his front porch, and cut the trail that won the Southwest.

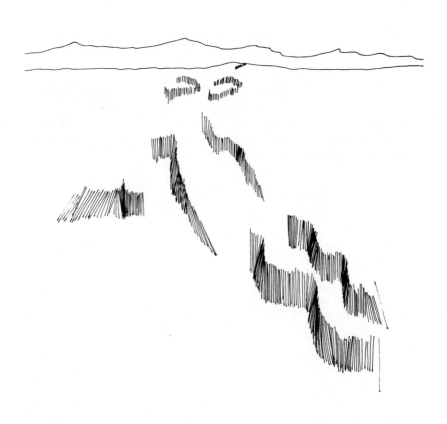

4

Hard Times: La Junta and Sand Creek

ON US ROUTE 50
heading east:
September 23

The last song from the jukebox died to the scrape of knives and forks on porcelain. I had pulled into one of those stalwart outposts of civilization, the cafe, and this one of whitewashed cement and hiding behind a faded Quaker State sign, saluted in isolation the caravans of trucks and cars heading east and west. Here in the Southwest it is downright un-American to stop anywhere else. Like Fort Laramie and Bent's Fort (just down the road) cafes sprout up along the highway to seduce, feed, and waylay. The great stories of the world are told over their formica tables, stories of the road and the range, and significant real estate deals are examined as scrupulously as Magna Cartas in their smoky corners.

I sank down into a corner chair and ordered eggs and waffles—always a safe bet on an untested menu. The place was sprinkled with ranchers, travelers, giggling boys, and proper girls: knots of people in idle conversation.

By ten-thirty I had finished my meal and had turned to get up when a lanky young man of twenty-five walked to the middle of the floor and asked the group:

"Anyone going to Las Animas?"

It had the inflection of being asked before on another morning. For a moment there was no beat to the music. Everyone sipped his or her coffee, boots crossed, and looked straight ahead. A few turned to the thin man in the barren center of the floor, while others stared blankly at their plates, stirring pools of jam or gingerly picking at their eggs.

Again the man's eyes swept around the floor:

"Come on, somebody's gotta be going that way."

Again silence.

I got up. He was dressed casually but nicely, and his eyes appeared gentle over large cheekbones. His finger hooked a windbreaker on his shoulder.

"I am," I said, directly to him. He walked over to my table. "But on one condition," I added. We sat down and toothpicks were offered and accepted.

"Oh, oh!" The man said. "What is it?"

"That you take me to someone who lived around La Junta in the mid-to-late-thirties . . . preferably when they were a child."

It seemed a rather strange stipulation, even to me when I said it. The man, called Mark, looked past me for a moment, the dark eyes holding steady on the windows in thought. He shook his head, but he wasn't declining my offer.

"Hmmm. Hiram Hall won't do. Hmmm. How about Grace McCory? Yes, the family's known her since we used to live outside La Junta a few years ago. She'd be in her fifties by now—a real talker, but no ones knows the parts like her."

Done. I took care of the bill and we headed for the Jeep, which I had unconsciously aimed down Parkman's exit route on the Arkansas River. We climbed in and drove into the rising sun.

We pushed down the seamed highway past farmhouses and open rolling hills fringed in cottonwoods. We drove through Fowler and Rocky Ford, busy with cantaloupe trucks, and we talked about eastern Colorado. Mark, I learned, was a history major at Southern Colorado and had become one of those unique sorts—one who knows more about his own state than about the history of Sri Lanka or Ireland.

By noon we had pierced the heart of one of the great agricultural regions of the Southwest, the Arkansas Valley, and had entered La Junta. It was a shy place, full of prim Victorian cottages set on letter-sized front lawns. There were cafes, bars, and ubiquitous Ford trucks piled with baled hay heading for the range. We crossed the Arkansas and headed north into fertile rectangles of land.

We came into country alternately blistered by sun in summer and ravaged by wind in winter. The soil, reddish-brown, part of the entisol group, reaches its northern limit in eastern Colorado. It is a young undeveloped soil, prey to drought, wind, and overgrazing, which in the thirties turned the landscape into a shifting, violent sea around La Junta and Lamar. That transformation of these fertile beds to the Dust Bowl of the Great Depression also destroyed lives and heritages. Farms collapsed, towns died, empires fell, psyches exploded, families gathered together and became snapshots of life on the road: grizzled young men, shoeless boys, resigned grandfathers, desperate mothers, and confused daughters leaning against loaded Dodges and Chevys aimed at the West Coast. Hundreds left here during the thirties, headed south, and picked up fabled Route 66—that retread of the Santa Fe Trail—and lurched through the New Mexico and Arizona deserts down into the lush corridor of the Pacific coast.

There were few reminders of that debacle, however: the fields appeared scoured and new as if they were tacked down over the wasted hills and dry creek beds of the past. White farmhouses stood erect and proud, outlined by clean picket fences. By the time we reached the McCory farm it was raining lightly; the clouds had dropped like a soft blanket and become tangled in the trees and the hills. Crows circled below the gray pall and dispersed in erratic formations.

I noticed the house first of all—a fragile but substantial yellow, frame cottage with a wide veranda, full of history in its chairs and tables. Cottonwoods spread out their branches over the roof and secured the house from sun and snow. We went up to the door and rapped on it three times. There were introductions, smiles, amid a committee of dogs and a calico. I noticed immediately the bond between Mark and Grace McCory.

Grace pulled us inside. The rain began to drum on the roof as we settled into a drawing room with chintz curtains and a piano that I knew had not been played for a very long time. While Mark scouted the refrigerator, I asked Grace, now part of an enormous armchair, about 1938.

There was a moment of recollection and breathing and then:

"I hated that year. I was ten years old. People in La Junta remember it well too. It was the worst year in this part of Colorado."

Mark entered the doorway bearing a ham sandwich, then leaned against the jamb, nibbling half-sentiently at his substantial lunch. He didn't look at me; he stared at Grace McCory with the kind of attention that I've seen people give saints, philosophers and video screens.

"As I said, I was ten. In April 1938, I lived about five miles from here, over that way. One afternoon I was coming home from school with my girl friends. It started out a lovely day—bright and sunny—but as I walked down the road the sky darkened behind me. I had my new dress and shoes on and an old haversack I used to carry books in hung from my elbow. The sky darkened, not with clouds but with thick dust. I'd seen dust storms before but this one soon covered the entire sky. All of a sudden, there was no sun, only rushing, blowing sand.

"The girls panicked and I became separated from them. I couldn't see more than twenty or thirty feet around me. I started to run blindly—across gulleys, creeks, and fields. I became terrified of the sound of the sand and the feel of it in my mouth and ears. I screamed and froze for a moment, right in the middle of a field. I couldn't move a finger."

It stopped raining. Mark had sat down and laced his fingers over his mouth. Suddenly the silence grew profound, so that the hum of the refrigerator switching on in the kitchen crackled through the room.

"Everything happened so quickly after that. Right in the same field not twenty feet away was an old Ford truck—sitting right on the dirt with no wheels. I crawled and scratched my way towards it and then got in the front seat. The wind was blowing like crazy. I tried to roll up the window but the window crank broke off in my hand. The sand blew through the front seat like somebody was heaving buckets of it from outside. There I was with all this protection from the sand and wind—and nothing would work. It seemed like a cruel miracle at the time. I wanted to cry and give

up. But I didn't. Don't ask me why, but that one moment I chose
to do something else— and live. It was a desperate attempt to
keep the sand off my head, to breathe and see: I put my haversack over my head and buried my head in the crack of the front
seat. I pushed my head as far in as I could. For two hours the
storm blew and I held tight in the dark—me in the haversack and
wedged in a small crack of the old Ford.

"Well, I got through the storm and through that year and the
next, though it was hard on daddy. The old Ford went to the
junkyard years ago, but I still remember it fondly.

"To this day I can pick books off the shelf, or take clothes out
of storage and shake out sand from 1937, 1938, and 1939. It came
in doors, windows, chimneys. It came and it stayed. I could grow
a geranium in the sand that I could shake from this old house."

That night I drove Mark to Las Animas, congratulating myself
about the stroke of luck that I had in finding him rideless in a
roadside cafe. As the Jeep scampered out of the wet streets of the
city, I also thought of Grace McCory and knew that the elements
that combine to make a great person in a noteworthy civilization
had conspicuously reappeared.

OFF STATE ROUTE 96:
September 24

The road into the heart is the loneliest road of all. Of the many
places I had to see, this one I dreaded the most. Sand Creek. It
has sad tonnage to it—a notation for overkill, cruelty, and waste.

Standing amid sparse cottonwoods, laced by Big Sandy Creek,
the site of the massacre, just north of Chivington, sabotages all
complacency and disarms the most experienced traveler. The
facts of the annihilation can be stated bluntly thus:

In November 1864, about five months before Lee's surrender
at Appomattox in Virginia, 750 troops under the command of
John Chivington left Fort Lyon (near Las Animas on the Arkansas
River) and marched northward. They encountered the Cheyenne
and Arapahoe village of Sand Creek that evening and prepared

an attack. A howitzer battery augmented the troops' assault. Chivington's forces moved in on the village on November 29, and following his orders, took no prisoners. The village of about 650 people was decimated—old men, women, and children, who comprised more than half the number of people in the camp, were murdered indiscriminately.

When you look at the facts and review the statements of the principal figures, you simply discover that no justification on earth exists for the wanton slaughter. If you're looking for more of an answer, however, try probing the enormous license taken into the field by invading armies and their commanders. For those who march, for us all, murder is embedded in the mind like a fault; suddenly ages wind down to the instant when the fissure widens and explodes.

I pushed the Jeep along Big Sandy Creek and parked on the rise just above the encampment—how vulnerable the spot looked below. There was a couple from Michigan in a VW van poking around when I got to the parking area. The man seemed genuinely perplexed by the crudeness of the massacre site, and as we peered down at the tarp of grass, weeds, wild flowers, and towering cottonwoods, he remarked to me:

"Hell, it doesn't look like anything happened here." He seemed like a garrulous but nice little man, who saved all his anger and confusion for fellow travelers. His wife, sacrosanct, hugged the door and whistled through her teeth absentmindedly. "Last summer," he resumed, "we went to Gettysburg. It was well marked with nice grass, white houses, fences, and cannons all around it. It *looked* like a battle was fought there; know what I mean? Maybe somebody could put up a marker or something here so people could kinda get an idea of where the battle was fought."

I smiled at his perfectly reasonable confusion.

"Yes, but this is the West," I answered at length. "The Little Big Horns, the Wounded Knees, the Sand Creeks are pretty much left as they were. Maybe the less modern reminders we have, the more we can rely on our imaginations."

We walked down into the valley, and upon returning to the Jeep I thought how I had surprised myself with this adroit comparison, and how much I had sounded like a spokesman for a government agency in need of a prompt and impressive explanation.

In truth, I could have used an insignificant marker by the road with mileage on it to the nearest gas station. Surely there must be one at Gettysburg.

5

The Santa Fe Trail
and Ludlow

The Santa Fe Trail. The very name has swat to it. Five sylla-
bles which summon up—and sum up—a generation of conflict, commerce, and exploration on the southern plains. Its
travelers were neophytes like Francis Parkman; mountain
men like Jim Beckwourth, "Broken Hand" Fitzpatrick, and
Jim Bridger; soldiers like Stephen Kearney; and modern va-
grants like Alfred Damon Runyon, who fled the offices of the
Pueblo Chieftain for a life on the rails, and ended up on
Broadway and the Bowery.

The Santa Fe Trail began in Missouri, a thin seam of dirt
connecting the Mississippi ports with the Spanish culture in
Santa Fe, New Mexico. The first branch, the "Cimarron Cutoff," exited Kansas's southwest border with Oklahoma and
entered northeast New Mexico. The second branch, the
"Mountain Branch," followed the Arkansas River into Colo-

rado and Bent's Old Fort, and just below La Junta, turned toward Trinidad, Raton Pass, and finally joined the "Cimarron Cutoff" below Fort Union east of the Sangre de Christos in New Mexico.

The fort's builders were Robert, Charles, William, and George Bent, and a partner, Ceran St. Verain. They quickly saw a need for an outpost on the Arkansas between Kansas and Santa Fe, and so in 1828 construction began on a site north of the Arkansas River. Fort William (original name) became Fort Bent: a medieval-looking, turreted leftover, measuring 180 feet long by 135 feet wide and whose adobe walls, strengthened with wool, are four feet thick.

By 1840 Bent's Fort attracted trappers, Indians, plainsmen, scouts, vagabonds, and mountain men—in short the lusty, colorful parade of Western man marching West. Kearney's Army of the West paused in 1846, as did Price's forces in 1847. With the steady decline of trade, however, the fort was abandoned by 1852 and William Bent, after several other business ventures, retired to a little ranch on the Purgatoire River.

Writers dream of inns and islands. Bent's Old Fort, its pale walls standing in the khaki grass, fulfills part of that requirement. Inns and islands have always served as restrictive microcosms. Characters meet in and on them, talk and disagree, fight against their walls and their shores, and like Chaucer's Canterbury pilgrims on a spring night, disturb the universe with their words.

I have heard it said that all the conversations uttered by people since day one are collected in a layer of the upper atmosphere. There, hovering in the sky, are Plato's lectures mingling with Leonardo's debates with himself, Aquinas's prayers bumping into Hitler's vitriolic speeches. If that is true, then I'm sure the walls of Bent's Fort have sent skyward remarkable dialogues for posterity: scout's tales; Jim Bridger's stories of the backwoods; Easterners' tales of the endless prairies and dangers of the frontier; a child's memories of creaking wheels, lightning, bison, Pawnee, and heat.

These old thick walls still have the power to move, although the conversations had departed generations ago and on that afternoon I only heard them in faint whispers.

By one in the afternoon the fort was a ghost on the prairie. From a short distance, its crudeness, suddenly apparent, I thought it looked straight from Beau Geste, lonely and deserted and invitingly mysterious. I then rejoined the Santa Fe Trail which parallels Highway 350. The Jeep bounced over the pavement and clung to the hot tar. I headed southwest toward Trinidad, accompanied by an apron of sagebrush and mesquite made even more desultory by its evenness.

ON THE PURGATOIRE RIVER:
September 27

Jeep owners can appreciate how the events of the morning unfolded.

The Jeep is a high vehicle, designed that way to cross rugged terrain and clear enormous rocks. To aid a normal person in getting into it, steps were installed on the driver's side, extending four inches out and acting like stirrups.

I had arrived the previous night and camped in a tent a few feet from the Jeep and close to the river. But a glorious night and a sky peppered with stars drove me out about three in the morning, and I slept between tent and tires. At six-thirty the world fidgeted and yawned and stretched around me; the sun inflated in the sky; a crow screamed in the chill air. That alarm forced my eyes open, and on impulse, my head bolted up and hit that metal stirrup with conviction.

Briefly the valley reverberated. The river departed. The sun danced like a piece of candy. When I gained my senses, I carefully rolled clear of any obstruction and staggered to my feet. I nursed my head over breakfast, cursing the half-baked ideas of car designers. Later I would retrieve the first-aid kit that always was so conveniently buried by a heap of clothes and shoes in the backseat.

My meal, a sordid combination of dried fruits and nuts, saw me through the coming of the lark bunting and the morning animation of the river. Purgatoire. PUR-ga-TWAH: to cleanse. The English verb *to purge* is derived from it. Its name has malice to it, as if every soul who witnesses its eddies must show some kind of penitence. Actually it is quite tame as rivers go, except for some furious bends downstream. The name is a French corruption of the Spanish El Rio de Las Animas Perdidas en Purgatorio (the River of the Souls Lost in Purgatory). A Spanish expedition from Mexico was massacred on its banks by Indians in the late sixteenth century—and as the group contained no priests to administer last rites, it was assumed their souls wandered forever in limbo.

The sun gained muscularity and line as it moved out of the wet haze of the prairie. An arrow of geese passed overhead, each movement in the pattern appearing part of a unique clockwork. Then all my hosts departed. The lark bunting sang in another part of the prairie; the geese winged to South America; even the crow that woke me into pain and frenzy (or simply an impostor) saucily banked and flirted above the river. The sun flooded the plain. By the time I had packed the Jeep it was well past nine and I pulled out, following the Purgatoire to Trinidad. At noon, the sun, a steady, brilliant saucer, saw me enter little Ludlow just off the Interstate.

Ludlow, like Antietam or Chickamauga in the East, would have remained an innocuous Colorado town were it not for the events of 1913-14. Those events began and ended, not with a lightning series of causes and effects, but like so much of history, with a process, slow in its metabolism, which involved staunch allegiances, furious debates, sporadic scrimmages, long intermissions, nervous truces, but very little action.

The so-called Ludlow Massacre took place on April 20,
1914, and grew out of a decade of hostility between miners and mine operators in the Ludlow-Walsenburg area. Since 1864 coal had been mined in southern and northern Colorado, and up until 1899, with the infiltration of the United Mine Workers Union, labor troubles accompanied the boom in the industry. Tensions increased as the miners and the union demanded strict eight-hour days and closer observance of mining laws. By the summer of 1913, the disagreement had mushroomed to the point that the miners' union declared a strike, shutting down the area mines and crippling production. Close to 10,000 miners and their families left their homes, and on cold drizzling afternoons packed their belongings into makeshift tent cities erected by the union. Eventually the Colorado militia was called in to control tempers and restore order. The standoff continued into 1914, and on April 20 it reached flashpoint. Taunted by angry strikers, the militia, poised in formation with rifles and two machine guns, fired into the sprawling tent colony. Five miners, one child, and one militiaman died from gunfire; two women and eleven children suffocated when militiamen torched the strikers' tents.

By the following month it became apparent that something was happening in Ludlow that was much more than a mob of strikers skirmishing with the militia and a handful of mine operators. To Upton Sinclair, the champion of the tyrannized and dispossessed, who in his classic novel *The Jungle* exposed the evils of the meat packing industry, it was an event of universal proportion. Ludlow, following the events of 1913 and 1914, became a watchword for rebellion, struggle, and protest among organized workers nationwide. Sinclair, long the supporter of groups without spokespeople, jumped into the thick of things in May 1914.

Just after the Ludlow incident, Sinclair hopped a New York train bound for Denver, infuriated by the fact that New York papers had given the Ludlow affair a scant column inch of coverage. He pounded out his assault on the press: "Our newspapers do not represent public interests, but private interests . . . they value a man, not because he is great, or good, or wise, or useful, but because he is wealthy or of service to vested wealth." Sinclair laid the blame for the Ludlow Massacre securely at the feet of the most prominent figure in Eastern politics and the single most important person in Western mining, John D. Rockefeller, Jr.

Sinclair arrived in Denver and immediately began marshaling public and political support to obtain a fair settlement of the miners' grievances. He roared in with a jack-the-giant-killer enthusiasm, discovering his most important foe not to be Rockefeller, but the governor of Colorado, Elias M. Ammons, whom Sinclair labeled "a kindly man, in intellectual caliber fitted for the duties of a Sunday School superintendent in a small village."

What incited Sinclair's rancor was Ammons's inability to settle the situation at the state level. Sinclair accused the governor of selling out to the mine operators, and even duping President Woodrow Wilson into leaving federal troops (in addition to the state militia) in the Ludlow area to prolong the strike. Moreover, Sinclair charged that Ammons was trying to prevent Wilson from forcing in compromise in the strike, and in stalling, the governor was pressing to break the strikers' will and coerce the miners back to work.

Sinclair raced back and forth between the state legislature and the *Rocky Mountain News,* surprised there to learn that the Associated Press was suspiciously silent on the strike's progress. He smelled a conspriacy to suppress information and block any continuing negotiations to end the dilemma. Throughout Denver he stumped for miners' rights, persistently encountering journalistic and political roadblocks. Even Upton Sinclair, renowned voice of the oppressed, felt the sting of organized political resistance, manipulated, he assumed, by the controller of the Colorado Fuel and Iron Company, John D. Rockefeller.

By June 1914, federal troops had restored order in Ludlow. Sinclair limped back to New York, still fuming about the press's irresponsibility, but knowing that the Ludlow showdown was to instigate serious policy changes between mining companies and unions.

In a way what Sinclair had dubbed "vested wealth" had won. But Ludlow, now tentless and naked in the low foothills of the Rockies, survives as a gritty reminder of the tenacity of small places to cling to the public imagination.

6

Sand and San Luis

U.S. ROUTE 160
September 28:

The landscape of southern Colorado is punctuated, if not dominated, by two magnificent summits: the Spanish Peaks. They rise above the buffalo grass and pine-studded ridges, snow slashed and hard blue against the pale sky. Their angles and shapes are particularly noteworthy. Viewed from the north they veer away from each other like two dancers, arms outstretched, their bodies held in perpetual tension. The peaks, like ragged and ancient fingers, meander toward the clouds.

But if the Spanish Peaks are elegant, Silver Mountain, to the right and looming through the windshield, has a shape that is both hypnotic and mystical. I can only compare it to the Great Pyramid, so smooth are it sides and so pronounced is its soaring peak. It is not an unusually high mountain. But its geometric profile arouses genuine emotions, emotions which in years' past have driven perfectly normal people great distances to worship such temples.

Its unnatural shape gives it a magic that no other mountain nearby can approach. The lowest hill anywhere can

share this power, if indeed its line can mesmerize the traveler. A rational painter such as Paul Cezanne spent a good
deal of his life analyzing the structure, shadows, and shapes
of a 3,300-foot limestone bluff called Mont. St. Victoire in
southern France. He could have chosen a loftier and snowier
summit, but he selected this innocuous ridge whose chame-
leon face churned his blood and stimulated his mind.

Such is Silver Mountain.

At this point a few words about the daily routine in the
mountains seem necessary. The Jeep provided not only
transportation, but also the means for an uncomfortable
sleep. I got up at seven nearly every morning, had breakfast
at eight, and was almost always on the road shortly thereafter. When I didn't drive, I'd extend breakfast to nine and
spend the mornings on long walks. I enjoyed these times as
much as I did the excursions into towns.

On walks into the mountains, I discovered the overwhelming complexity of nature swelling around me. It is so
complex and the mind is bombarded with so many diverse
images—leaves, branches, dead flowers, stems, bark, clouds—
that I've often thought of the forest as the grand contradic-
tion: it feeds so many pictures to the mind, but it is during
that moment of subtle confusion that we are capable of the
clearest thinking. In a stem must be concentrated the lugs
and pulleys of human thinking. The mind must not only
thrive on natural processes, but also depend on them.

I catalogued the plants, not with the diligent notational
skill of a botanist, but with the flypaper mind of an artist.
Sometimes I would set up my drawing board and study the
lines undulating in the curves of a flower. Here beautiful and
grotesque leaves take on geographies as different as warring
planets. Or as I simply walked through the woods, the mind,
persistently absorbing and jettisoning information, would
file away the most common or bizarre shapes of leaves and
flowers for future use. The funny thing was that I had no
control over what came and what stayed. Up there in the
brain is a different, diminutive person who counts, selects,

and files all the minutiae of the world we walk through, then
serves it back to us, unannounced, at the oddest times.

I would run every night about six, averaging about two miles a night. I didn't run to partake of the metaphysical or commune with the universal mind, but pretty much to stay in shape. And aside from the current health blitz I think the union of mind and body is essential to normal functioning. Besides, I admire people who do things for the love of doing them, no matter how eccentric they might sound. I heard of a man who started running five miles a day when he was fifty, long before such distances were common. Today at eighty he maintains the same pace through anything nature wishes to hurl at him.

Such as it is with amateurs. Bells do not ring or summit conferences convene when they lace up a pair of Adidas and take to the road. Real lovers don't need them. They simply slip out the back door and assume their responsibility that some people would call a punishment. Out on the tarmac or the footpath a particular battle is waged and won daily, with no audience or referees as witnesses.

I headed west, temporarily stopping in the mountains near the Spanish Peaks. But the traveler in Colorado quickly realizes that the mountains soon drop again into a vast prairie stretching seventy miles to the next mountain range. To the south is Spanish Colorado; to the northwest are the Great Sand Dunes. At Fort Garland I kept the Jeep on the road that eventually veered west and then due north into the arms of the Great Sand Dunes.

I suspect that people make special pilgrimages here to feel insignificant. Around me waves and waves of sand stretch in a vast sea toward an unnaturally rigid horizon. Some of the dunes tower fifteen hundred feet; under the sun you somehow feel that you have been dropped into a huge inland Egypt.

A soft breeze stirred the surface grains and a minor tornado whirled a foot off the ground, dancing away over the floor of sand. Under the leeside of the dune, the wind struggled, moaned, and then died. There was a nakedness to the shifting floor, unbroken by a blade of grass or promise of rain. By the middle of the afternoon, against a radiant sky, the colors of the sea had changed from beige to umber and then to purest blue and violet. By late afternoon the sides of the dunes were shot with scarlets and burgundies.

There were no clouds, only the confrontation of sand, sky, and sun. I was so close to the symbols of death that it felt curiously good to be alive.

The Sand Dunes form a pocket that tightly fits against the west wall of the Sangre de Christos. Beyond the dunes to the north and west stretches an undulation plain, which for thousands of years has allowed the sand to blow unimpeded till it reached the foot of the mountains. The sand originally formed the bed of a large inland sea; when the sea disappeared the prevailing westerly winds took care of the rest.

But myths are born in dreams and visions and not in fact. A strange legend has it that web-footed horses canter across the horizon on moonlit nights, their manes long, tossed, and flamboyant. Their webbed feet allow them to glide over the sand.

At three in the afternoon the southern Colorado sun has a dizzying effect. One can talk philosophically about deserts and the thrill of isolation, but one usually does it with a Jeep or a canteen of water nearby.

It was the artist who reclaimed the deserts after the explorer, rancher, and emigrant passed them by. No matter how brutal the desert seems, it is that starkness that makes us feel the most comfortable. It is nothing more than it appears to be. Its nakedness nourishes the soul and its lines echo the simple geometric truths that Euclid imparted to the ancient world. The desert is life uncomplicated. It resists all our technology and learning, stares at us with a mute and incorruptible face, and bears in its sands the concentration of mystery and time and human futility. And because the desert has little practical use, artists and poets are stuck with the responsibility of praising it.

It wasn't a vagabond artist but an advancing hiker who pulled me from my thoughts. He first appeared like a gaunt apparition plodding over the dunes, turbaned, clad in shorts and boots, and bearing his house on his shoulders. He quickly was in front of me, walking stick and legs in full mo-

tion. I gestured to speak to him, but presently I realized that
nothing would stop him.

"Where you headed?" I asked.

He puffed: "East. Walsenburg . . . you?"

"San Luis—then the Western Slope."

He smiled. "Ah, then we'll have to meet in heaven some day and compare notes." And he was gone, and I could only smile at his terse arrival and departure.

It was late afternoon when I left the Great Sand Dunes, turned south, and passed the low adobe walls of Fort Garland, signaling I was entering the territory of Spanish Colorado.

In summer, night truly falls. But in September it nibbles at the sky and finally swallows it shortly thereafter. The pavement from Fort Garland to San Luis, San Pablo, and Chama is as straight as a string. It threads the narrow gap in the Sangre de Christos and runs through sand as dry as corn flakes, spangled with arid lakes, irrigated fields, and clusters of greasewood.

This is Coronado's Colorado, a section of the state in which the remnants of the Spanish explorer's army settled well into the nineteenth century. We have inherited a love of the road from the Spanish. They first ventured out in the fifteenth and sixteenth centuries, seeking everything from gold to territory. They broke free from the staleness of European living and championed exploration and discovery. By the eighteenth century, educated men were well-traveled men. It was incumbent for a young man to tour Europe and absorb the cultures of France, Italy, Switzerland, and Germany. The university education was only as sufficient as the miles spent afterward, studying the manners of Paris, the vistas of the Grand Chartreuse, and the arts of Rome.

So the road goes on. Here in this barren valley, swept by the Spanish conquistadors, the need for exploration and discovery continues, even among the dry roots and the lumbering vegetable trucks. And the common rearview mirror, which frames a Mack truck grill or Mercedes star, is more representative of the American experience than most paintings in the museums of the country.

It was pitch-dark when I pulled up to the pumps of a little

gas station in San Luis. I heard a man talking in Spanish to a woman, then he swung past the hood of the Jeep and touched his straw hat.

"Feel 'er up, señor?"

I said yes, to the top, and I got out and stretched in the young night. The lights were just being switched on across the town, and suppers were brewing under them.

"This the oldest town in Colorado?" I asked.

"Oldest in Colorado, si." He smiled, and not knowing how to proceed further, watched the pump dial tick off the numbers. Finally he asked:

"Where are you going, señor? Taos? Santa Fe?"

"No," I replied. "*Here.*"

For a moment the man reflected. I could sense the flash-cards falling one by one in his mind of the highlights and attractions of his small town. He then became perplexed.

"*Here,* señor?" And he shrugged his shoulders, took my money, and shuffled off inside. I then heard a brief burst of Spanish and then nothing but the sounds of the night.

As I was just about to pull out, I heard a loud swelling "Señor!"

The self-elected ambassador of San Luis came running up to the Jeep and waved a bright piece of paper.

"You need a map, no?"

"Yes. How much?"

"Fifty cents." I gave him a dollar and he beamed with the satisfaction of someone sending a gypsy in the right direction.

I had a sufficient amount of maps, but there are no such things on earth as an extra map and an overly detailed one. On the contrary, most people who travel with the skimpiest directions reach their destinations through blind luck. An average map will give you an accurate lay of the land, town population, and so forth. But a great map tells the motorist if the right turnoff comes *before* the town or *after.* A misplaced road, even in size the width of an eyelash, can have him or her discovering the wrong end of the continent.

I checked this one out while idling in the driveway. It was a jewel. I could have been surveying Eden, so detailed were the roads, so accurate the reliefs. I had originally decided to ferret out a motel, but armed with this new information I drove out of San Luis, sped past the stores hugging the street, and headed for the Rio Grande.

It was dark and silent. My thumb followed a dirt road on the map, and I was on it shortly thereafter. It was bumpy but I lurched through it, yo-yoing back and forth, the Jeep's engine heaving and sputtering as it wallowed in each fresh rut. I knew that I was due west of San Acacio, and the river was dead ahead.

I flashed my high beams and kept the Jeep close to the road. Some ten minutes later, after being tossed silly, I could hear over the engine the steady pulse of the Rio Grande. I slowed, thanked the ambassador at the pumps, and the mapmaker with the good eye.

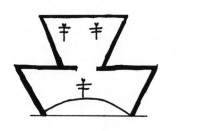

7

To The Mesa

BELOW WOLF CREEK PASS
September 30:

The Rio Grande begins in the San Juan National Forest, swings into a graceful comma at Del Norte and flows south into the uplands of New Mexico. I reached the south fork of the river and camped near Beaver Creek, just east of the Continental Divide.

I was back in the mountains again, and somewhat concerned that the cloudless weather would soon change. The following morning the first gray clouds appeared, but they seemed only to soften the sun and not obscure it.

That morning I made two discoveries: the first was that the Jeep clutch seemed abnormally loose, and the second was that an aspen leaf explained the drainage of the western United States.

At nine o'clock I was pondering the fate of the Jeep. And when you don't want something to go wrong you will generally convince yourself that nothing will. The clutch did not have the proper tension. I looked; I doubted; I probed and tested. And soon I determined that it could make the rest of the trip, and not to shove any bad fortune into the problem when nothing appeared calamitous.

I forgot, for the moment, my doubts about the Jeep by taking a long walk among the great stands of spruce, fir, and aspen. On a small rise I sat down, and studying a fallen aspen leaf I explained to myself the Continental Divide and the drainage east and west of the creeks, brooks, and rivers.

On a yellow, brittle little map not two inches across is the microcosm of the Rockies and Great Plains: the Continental Divide is a high ridge from which gravity on the left pulls things south and west; on the other side, like the veins in the leaf, is a similar conformity with the pull drawing things east and south.

I returned to the campsite about eleven and noticed that I had company. A monstrous camping rig had pulled into a spot not fifty yards away. Generally these lumbering hulks spell danger, for often platoons of screaming kids pass out of their portals and infiltrate the innocent forest. But this one was silent.

I decided to break the ice. After getting within thirty feet of the camper, I saw the door pop open and out stepped a man in his midfifties. I suppose he had been keeping his eye on me through the curtain. I thought of a silly question that afterwards seemed even more ludicrous.

"Did you come from the west," I asked, "through the pass?"

"Yeah. Sure did."

"Is it open?"

Of course it was open. I knew it was open. Everyone in Colorado knew it was open. But I had to say something.

Then a boy of perhaps twelve appeared in the open doorway, his Bronco's hat askew, and sat down on the step only a few yards behind the man. In the boy's eyes there leaped a hidden struggle in a very confident but unsmiling face.

The man said: "This here's Charlie."

We left the boy in the doorway. The man guided me a short distance to a crude picnic table. The man looked back at the boy.

"Charlie's not going to talk much," he said to me. "But I could do with a little of it myself. Been on the road a few days—we're going up to the Bronco game this Sunday, Charlie and me."

I observed that Charlie looked a little pale.

The man reflected for a moment, then he said:

"Charlie's got leukemia. We do the best we can. He always wanted to go up and see the Broncos play. So me and Charlie are gonna do it. RIGHT CHARLIE?"

We spent the next fifteen minutes discussing Charlie's condition and speculating on how much hope there was of a successful treatment of the disease. I suppose I made the mistake of assuming that the man was the boy's father, for he quickly cor- rected me.

"No, I'm not Charlie's dad. I'm just a neighbor. You see, Charlie's dad works in an auto body shop. Well, he can't get much time off, so we on the block pitch in whenever we can. This week's my turn. Charlie's a great companion—that's what makes it fun."

Somehow any of my problems at that point seemed comparable to a territorial revolt on Neptune.

I left the next morning for Mesa Verde, and saw the immense rig with Charlie in the jump seat head out for Denver and a big, big game.

From Beaver Creek the road ascended to Wolf Creek Pass and dropped in a wide spiral into Pagosa Springs. For many years Pagosa Springs was the center of a dispute between the warring Utes and Navaho. Now it occupies a peaceful rectangle of land bounded by the San Juan Forest and the Ute reservation on the south.

From Pagosa Springs to Mesa Verde, the road descended from the mountains into the rolling plateaus of southwestern Colorado. Then at Bayfield the land became flat and dry, and I passed the rivers draining from the west side of the Continental Divide: Los Pinos, Florida, Las Animas, and La Plata. And just after I crossed the Mancos River I could barely see the high tables of Mesa Verde.

CHAPIN MESA
September 30:

This is no country for old men. People wander here to die or to dream. The same sun that splashes Paris and bathes Venice here pummels people and vegetation. Due south the New Mexican desert stretches to Mexico, a wrinkled elephant skin of pinched, forested ridges and scarred *arroyos,* dimpled by two great rivers, the Rio Grande and the Pecos, sweeping down in parallel curves into the sand kiln of the southern border. Rattlesnakes squirt over the sand, Spanish bayonets prick the dry air, and the sky stays a cruel blue.

From the first minute you step onto the mesa you are held by the brutal severity of sand and piñon, split by canyons which snake to the arc of the earth. The large sandstone ledges made natural protective awnings for the first Mongoloid hunters who wandered into this region 12,000 years ago. The earliest permanent settlers, the Basketmakers, flourished for close to 500 years, then quite inexplicably, their culture was replaced by the cliff-dwelling Pueblos who thrived here well into the thirteenth century.

The Pueblos were responsible for erecting the enormous and intricate cliff fortresses at Mesa Verde. And in a way, the dwellings are a primitive response to those who decry the closeness of apartment living. The truth is that early in the development of Pueblo culture, the relative compactness of the cliff houses fostered a deeper unity among the residents.

By modern standards they appear crude and inhospitable. But as far as being functional architecture, they set a rare pace. No other domestic architecture to my knowledge takes more advantage of inaccessibility for protection, and selects its position with such concern for sun in winter and shade in summer. The cliff houses are superb models of the primitive mind and demonstrate clearly that the past produced some gifted artists, engineers, visionaries, and city planners.

The rooms of the dwellings are windowless and quite small, averaging eight by ten feet, which has led some to believe that the Pueblo were short in stature. Actually, they were not abnormally small, but spent so little time in enclosed rooms that they restricted the interior's verticality. The doors are narrow and low. The roofs are constructed of heavy poles placed over the walls, with final layers of mud plaster inserted to ensure adequate insulation. An average building site contains fifty million stones and thousands of poles and beams.

The life of the community took place in the open court and on terraced roofs. When the men were not working, they perhaps spent their late afternoons in the *kivas*—the imposing round chambers specifically built for ceremonial and religious use. There is speculation on the nature of the religious rites. But as in other similar cultures, religion is probably tangled with the need to hunt successfully, plant crops, and have children.

By the beginning of the last quarter of the thirteenth century, nature, which perenially shows an indifference to our wishes, stopped smiling on the people of Mesa Verde. A severe drought began, persisted, and ultimately destroyed the grand community on Mesa Verde.

Art was a way of trying to control the problem of the drought and was something like a visual prayer for the adverse weather to cease. The Pueblo, and other primitive (historically, not intellectually) cultures, believed that the image of something had magical powers. The cave paintings in Altimira, Spain, sprung from a similar belief—the frescoes of deer and bison were meant to insure an adequate hunt.

The art that developed from this last phase of the Pueblo culture at Mesa Verde was highly agitated and symbolic. The symbols used by the artists are supercharged with meaning because they are the lanuage of the soul trying to communicate with the forces beyond. The symbol is the prayer. Consequently, the symbols of rain, clouds, rainbows, lightning bolts, mountains, are merged with symbols of creatures found *near* water, such as tadpoles and dragonflies, which strengthen the artist's prayer to the gods. The gods seemingly are captivated by the artist's ability to imitate so well their creations. So, as the artist believes, to draw well is to sit in the lap of the gods and have a private hearing.

The Pueblo artist is not the rebel as in nineteenth-century European painting. He or she seeks not conflict, but union and does not wish to attack society, but to praise and protect it. The artist is the synthesizer of culture, the vessel into which the society pours its hopes, fears, and dreams. As a kind of pictorial lobbyist, the artist furthers his or her culture's cause by implementing and refining the visual language that he or she reveals to the gods. In one sense, the artist is the intercessor between the aspirations of human beings and the pliable will of the gods.

But then, unpredictably, in the fatal last quarter of the thirteenth century, all the symbols failed and the skies grew silent.

In 1295, the year Marco Polo returned to Venice from the Orient, and the year Dante was thirty, a young Pueblo brave stretched out in the midday sun and tried to make sense of it all.

He was twenty-six. He had a wife and a boy of ten. He was an artist and a good hunter.

For a moment he lingered in the warm sun and dreamed of the time when he was a young boy, and times were good. Now the beans and squash were shriveling up on the mesa tops. Even the juice of the delicious prickly pear did not trickle down your chin. For a very long time the sun had baked the mesa, and even the *kivas* had grown stifling and full of stench.

He wanted to die and let the sun shrivel him, too.

Presently he got up. The sun blinded him at first, but then he managed to squint and look south over the barren tables of sand. The wind murmured and seemed to carry his low spirit out to the horizon.

With the next sun he would leave. He would take his wife and son and head south toward the rain and better crops. The sun would follow them, but soon the clouds would come in that fresh new land.

Many times he had seen his people leave. They left and never came back. They moved south through the valleys, through the piñon and cactus, toward the sun.

Once he had defended his home against the enemy. They had dropped from the cliffs and he had slain them on his doorstep. He had felt courageous. He had crafted the stone tips of his own arrows. He had met the enemy and won.

But this was different. This silent enemy gripped your soul. There was nothing to fight. The sun and the sand pummeled you. You didn't feel like a man.

He retraced his steps over the mesa. He saw advancing toward him a younger man from his own house. The younger man wanted to know if he could join the artist and his family on their journey.

This sudden brotherhood warmed the artist. So they would put their fortunes on the line and leave together.

They walked to the edge of the mesa, and their eyes turned to the southeast. Under the rim of the adjoining mesa was the impressive palace, now in a long shadow.

The young artist felt a pain deep inside. He would leave the mesa, his house, and *kiva*, and most of all he would leave the palace that held his father's paintings. It was there he was taught his art—taught the brilliance of symbols and shown the techniques of mixing water and hematite.

So it would have to be.

The sun never felt as treacherous or as unforgiving.

An errant vulture in the summer of that year might have witnessed a strange sight: two young men, a boy, and and woman plodding through the sand and heat with obvious dedication,

heading in the direction of the rising sun. The vulture played on   51
drafts of wind, turned his wings to the sun and swooped lower.   *To the*
Below him the wasteland, the hard canyons exposed like bare   *Mesa*
bones, quivered in the heat.

It couldn't have known—it was an innocent bird, mortal—but it beheld the last migrations of the Pueblo in Colorado. The bird watched the figures move against the sand and scrub, and once convinced their legs were not faltering, banked, and turned west over the Colorado Plateau. The artist saw its dark wings depart, but he also turned, not west but south, to where the sun hung in the sky like a beacon.

The artist, his family, and friend perhaps made it as far as Chaco or even Acoma, but most likely they were absorbed by the Rio Grande pueblos, where their children's children witnessed the arrival of Coronado and viewed the perpetual cinema of misunderstanding, murder, and retribution, that accompanied the Pueblo and Spanish cultures into the twentieth century.

By 1310, the cliff houses of Mesa Verde were empty. The wind blew across the discarded pots and bowls, infiltrated the *kivas*, and forced dust into the corners where young braves once curled into sleep. Like skeletons, they now face the anatomist.

Late that afternoon, after pursuing a tourist mob and a park ranger up and down more ladders than I care to remember, I went out to the mesa and stretched out under the sun in the same place the young artist, centuries ago, had lain and deposited his dreams. I don't think anyone saw me perform this little ritual, and at that point, I didn't care if they did.

Drought had beaten him: it could have been an earthquake, famine, or something insignificant like a rattlesnake or lightning. But no, the clouds eluded the Colorado Plateau, and the skies remained brilliant through rainless summers. I dug my back into the sand and felt the slap of sun and the rub of wind.

In that moment when my sand silhouette passed into his, I felt his coming and his going, felt the hand paint the pots and cliffs of the mesa, and knew there was a complete, mystical indentification. I ran my hand through the sand, closed my eyes and saw the symbols, like orbiting moons, arc through my mind, symbols that are stronger than paint or sandstone or clay, and which move the world.

I wait alone till the plump sun goes down: a large orange cinder that turns the stones and trees to a violent rust color. The horizon is as straight as the line of sea meeting sky.

The sun slouches into silent benediction. I sit on a rock above the Pueblo graveyard spread out below. Almost every evening in the Southwest is apocalyptic, and we view it in grim ceremony. Perhaps we invest the dying sun and rising darkness with more meaning than is necessary. It is, after all, part of a continual and somberly repetitious cycle of sun, stars, snow, rain, drought, and flood.

Only mortal man sets up the meanings and omens.

But the Pueblo absorbed the heavens into their art. For a culture that depended so much on the moist skies and lush earth for its growth, it only seems natural that their art be tethered to the stars, the spinning galaxies, and the beating sun.

Night falls on the art and the roots and stones of the mesa. The sun rests like a slim fingernail on the purple earth. I get up, dust off my trousers, and prepare to rendezvous with a man I will call Carl.

I very much wanted to know how the mesas were being looted of their ancient pots and artifacts. The pillaging is rampant, and rangers are unable to control the problem. Imagine the Louvre or the British Museum with unguarded exits, and you can understand the porosity of the national parks like Mesa Verde. I particularly wanted to know how the professionals work. I wanted to know how someone could steal Pueblo art and smuggle it across the country to rest in the conservatory of a fashionable New York apartment. Most of all, though, I wanted to know why.

I meet Carl by his submarine-colored van. It is dusk. Carl has served time in prison for plundering artifacts in Hovenweep. Reluctantly, he has consented to re-create for me how he and others raided sites around the Colorado Plateau and removed Pueblo artifacts. He works coolly and with little emotion. Tonight I will go with him.

We wear Levi's, tennis shoes, and long-sleeved cotton shirts. Carl prepares the rope in the back of the van. He works diligently and saves the talk till we climb into the frontseats. He plays the scene as if it were real.

"Today I scouted an area near a tributary of the Mancos," he says. "That's where we are headed. Several pots, bowls, and junk."

"Junk?"

"Yeah—stuff that doesn't bring any money—bones, dolls, maybe some leather goods."

We drive along the mesa for about three miles, taking several dusty, single-lane roads. Carl stops the van on a wide shoulder of the road. We wait as darkness closes in.

"I never take the pots until I go back at night," he says. "I just look when I am about in the day."

I notice the bony fingers that drum on the wheel, and the gray eyes that dart nervously in the dying light.

We climb out of our seats and onto the pebbly shoulder. Carl ties a bandanna around his curly blond hair. He checks the flashlight.

"Who are you working for tonight?" I ask.

"A buyer in Miami and the middle man in Albuquerque. I go in and get the stuff, take it out, and contact the man in Albuquerque. We arrange shipment. The buyer is notified by phone. He makes a bid sight unseen."

"Isn't that a bit risky for the buyer?"

"The demand exceeds the supply. If he wants an original Anasazi pot, he puts up the money over the phone—period."

"You get your money from the man in Albuquerque?"

"Right. As soon as he receives the pottery, I get the other half of the money we originally agreed on."

"How much?"

Carl wipes his mouth with his sleeve. He does not say anything. Then:

"Five hundred, a thousand, depending on how hard the search, the type of pottery, condition, expenses—so forth."

"Pretty clinical, isn't it?"

"Yeah."

"Did you make a good living from this?"

"Pretty good."

"Do you know anything about the pots you're stealing?"

"No."

The night is quiet, and we are alone amidst the wildness. I wanted to ask him who the buyers were and why they bothered risking their necks in the black market trade. But I already knew the answer. It came to me as I waited by the side of the van. They had run out of cheap possessions like Rolls Royces and mansions. And art, because it is immortal, and because it is always greater than the person who owns it, is the ultimate possession. It is greater than gold, larger than life itself, the only route to the past.

It is pitch-dark. Carl knows the territory like his backyard. He takes the rope, a flashlight, and shuts the door of the van.

We leave the road and descend into a dry creek bed. Carl doesn't use the flashlight, but keeps it tucked into his back pocket. He has extraordinary night vision. I follow close behind, my eyes glued to the white ribbon he has tied above his elbow. Scrub and sage tear at my pantlegs. We do not talk. The wash is grainy and filled with small boulders the size of pearls that shift under our feet. Once or twice I look around. There are fidgetings in the night landscape: soft avalanches of sand from squirrels scurrying. We pass under ragged rocks lit only by a rain of stars. We seem to be continually descending, but I can't be sure.

We walk ten minutes. Carl suddenly raises his hand and stops dead in his tracks. His eyes flit over the small pale hills. He points right, so we turn and climb a little bluff studded with sage. We drop over two or three ledges, measuring only four to five feet in height. We are back up on top of a mesa, and the big dark sky broods over us. We come to the naked stone edge of a precipice.

We are alone, except for the stones and stars and the ghostly shapes of piñon. There is no sound.

Carl says: "Do you want me to go over first?"

"How far down is it?"

He peers quickly over the edge. "Maybe fifteen, twenty feet."

"No, I'll go," I finally whisper.

As he ties us together with bowlines, I begin to doubt my sanity. We are somewhere in the sprawling Colorado Plateau—where precisely, I have no idea.

I take the flashlight and drop over the edge, hooked only to Carl. I feel the coarse, cool sandstone slip from my fingers, and I descend gradually, bouncing on the balls of my feet. Carl feeds me more rope and I plunge inch by inch, foot by foot, till my toes feel the stone of the shelf under me. I land on both feet and tug twice on the rope.

I flash the light behind me: a cache of pots and bowls and

other obscure remnants appears in the steady beam. I catch my
breath. It doesn't appear touched since the fourteenth or thirteenth centuries. The smell of dust pervades. I can only stay a few
minutes, and emotion and the need to see everything is packed
into the passing seconds.

I shuffle over to the scattering of pots. I touch one, and feel the
hard, grainy earthiness of its rim—and six centuries of coldness
and darkness. My fingers linger on it. Then I turn out the light. It
is over. Its secret will forever be a part of me. The household
goods will rest eternally to wait for their owner's return, or for
other bandits to stumble on to them.

I signal Carl to pull me up. If I were a thief, I would be carrying
up a good haul tonight. But as it is, I carry up only the shirt on my
back—and a memory. I arrive at the top, Carl straining on the
rope.

"Well?" he puffs.

"They are there—just as you said."

"Piece a cake, huh?"

We get our breaths for a minute, curl up the rope, stow the
light, and head back over the mesa and the *arroyo.*

We are back in the van.

"Don't you ever feel perverse before or after any of these
raids?" I ask Carl.

"What do you mean?"

"Never mind."

We drive down the dusty winding road, heading north into the
vast dead space between the Big Dipper and the North Star. And
the earth is silent again after our going.

8

Ouray, Ouray

U.S. ROUTE 550
October 2:

The road north from Durango to Ouray snakes along the Las Animas River and winds slowly up into the San Juan Forest. There are roads that bore the happiest of people, and there are roads that steal your heart. But this one is a spiritual banquet—not just a highway but a separate journey of the mind—amid a sweep of aspen undulating against the dark green fir.

The aspen here are virtually a different species. They have a length and a majesty that make them special. Like a forest of elegant matchsticks thrown on end, they lean into the wind and take the drafts gracefully, their leaves shimmering and dancing.

The leaves are heavier than their soft stems causing them to tremble in the slightest breeze. One tree can be full of glorious motion; a whole stand is kinetic sculpture. Here mature aspens reach seventy to eighty feet, their long trunks exposed and their foliage rippled by wind.

Just before eleven in the morning I pulled into camp, some ten miles south of Ouray. The Jeep had behaved admirably: the clutch seemed rubbery but sound. I had carefully avoided garages, except for gas, relying mainly on the totem power of curses, prayers, and downright intimidation.

I unpacked the Jeep, pitched the tent, and after lunch I climbed a wooded slope to get a better view of Mount Sneffels.

We as mortals have always deified mountains simply by looking up to them. Of course mountains are the great symbols of power. From Mount Olympus, the lives and fortunes of Prometheus and Agamemnon were mechanically controlled; from Mount Sinai, the entire direction of Judeo-Christian thought was announced in stone. High places have directed the lives of the people of Athens, Fujiyama, Machu-Picchu, Sumeria, and Egypt. They have held in sway the most rational minds of Jerusulem, Mecca, and Assisi. Not to mention all the pilgrims who flock to the summits of Manhattan. Mountains are the natural temples through which we fulfill the need to supplicate ourselves. To challenge them requires rebellion. And once conquered, we partake of the power of the gods.

In myth and literature, mountains are the opposite of deserts as symbols. The latter are part of the tragic pattern: full of waste, isolation, and confusion. But mountains are usually symbols of quest. They hold objects that heroes desire. So off the hero goes through forests, fields, deserts, in quest of the fiery ruby at the summit. Up through the granite crags he pursues his way—the very obstacles in his path form part of the virtue of his search. When he reaches the top, ruby in hand, the quest is completed, the pattern of the myth fulfuilled. But, too, by reaching the top, he has usurped the power of the gods and now feels a bit greater than his mortal self. He must be on guard. For now his virtue must be tested and retested in a series of subsequent quests, usually with the mountain, castle, or temple as the major challenge.

The myth is given various settings and interpretations, but importantly, *good* is always in quest, and evil is always in resistance.

Mountains pass in and out of myth, literature and art—as psychological symbols they let us associate, even from a distance, with the pavilions of power and briefly allow us a glimpse at the immortal world.

Mount Sneffels appeared more like a mythical tower than a real mountain peak. But by early afternoon, clouds drifted

around its sheer walls and the temperature began to plunge.
Within a half hour the wind rose, scattering the dead leaves and stripping the trees of their remaining brittle stems.

The sky turned a deep, somber gray to the north, the wind howled, and the forest grew deathly silent. There was no one in sight.

I walked back to the Jeep and secured my gear in the frontseat. I could tell that snow was imminent.

I decided to turn the Jeep so that the engine faced south, away from the bite of the north wind. It was on a small slope, so I would have to back up a few yards and pull forward a few feet. The snow began to swirl. I got in, turned the key in the ignition, and shoved in the clutch. Then the inconceivable happened.

The small amount of tension involved in backing up the slope sent the lifeless clutch clear to the floor. I pumped a dead rubber arm. I put on the hand brake and grabbed the steering wheel. I then got out and looked under the engine behind the front wheel. The linkage arm dangled just clear of the pine needles on the dirt.

I crawled under the engine with a wrench and tried to reattach the linkage. Every time it popped in, the stress on the clutch shattered the bushing holding the linkage together.

It wouldn't work. After fifteen minutes, with the snow falling rapidly, I gave up. I got back in the Jeep and took stock of everything.

I was three miles off the highway. A storm was blowing through quickly. As far as I knew, I couldn't move the Jeep's gears without the clutch. I waited and thought.

I decided then and there to do nothing. It seemed in the blitz of possibilities the only thing to do. I would weather the storm and wait for morning.

It was five in the afternoon. When I got over feeling like Crusoe, I decided to prepare for the night and put the whole thing out of my mind.

I eased the Jeep onto a level spot, secured the hand brake, and got the inside ready to live in. I stowed all the gear in the frontseat, piled to the headliner. I spread out the sleeping bag with the top just beside the gears. Then I got in.

The temperature in the Jeep I guessed was around forty degrees. Outside, the snow danced, and a gray pall fell on the trees.

I nibbled on cheese and crackers and slipped into a dialogue with myself where disgust, futility, and rage became strangely mixed with a sense of elation. I felt as lost as a drifting cloud. Then the most delicious feeling of remoteness overcame me. I couldn't explain it, but it was near religious in its intensity.

I read till the natural light grew feeble in the window, and then I switched on the battery light and read some more. The wind blew, the trees moaned, and the snow swirled and fell like it had been shaken from all the planets in the heavens.

When I finally got to see Ouray it was from the frontseat of a tow truck. The next morning I had tramped to the highway, hitchhiked into town, and arranged for the tow.

It was a brilliant morning, but cold. The storm had passed, leaving a soft powder on the mountains.

I dropped the Jeep off at the garage about twelve and that afternoon did Ouray on foot.

The city is lodged between the big shoulders of the Uncompahgre National Forest. Within a year after rich silver deposits were discovered, Ouray was incorporated in 1876. It grew, boomed, and busted within twenty years, securing its tough reputation and losing much of its virtue.

But today there is a certain friendliness in the air of Ouray, a niceness that transcends its history and welcomes you to its sidewalks and doorways. In its pocket in the hills it *is* Gstaad for a brief moment, then declares its stubborn Western allegiance through its creosote-stained walls and bleached gray roofs.

If there was a personality to match the wildness of the Uncompahgres, it was found in the wiry little body of David Frakes Day. Certainly no one in Ouray has forgotten the stories surrounding Day and the publication of his daily, *the Solid Muldoon.*

The first issue hit Ouray September 5, 1879, and was named after an Irish fight promoter whom Day admired. From that day on, editorial journalism in this part of Colorado would be shaped by Day's biting sarcasm and irreverent wit. The *Muldoon* was notorious for including hearsay, gossip, libelous attacks, barbed harangues, and diatribes in addition to the news of the day. At one time, Day had over forty lawsuits pending against him; all were settled in his favor.

The fame of *the Solid Muldoon* stretched all the way to Europe. Once, while traveling in England in the 1800s, Day was presented to Queen Victoria. She became an admirer of Day's publication and eventually a loyal subscriber.

Day admitted to being "candid and impetuous," but his real savagery was reserved for politicians, hard-line mine speculators, and officials in general. Once in Durango, after fidgeting through the long-winded speech of a pompous senator, Day stretched his feet onto a chair in the front row and yawned. The senator apologized to Day for being a bit wordy. Day remarked, "Don't worry, Jim, we can lie down here as long as you can lie up there."

That night I slept in a motel bed because it was white and soft and there. Don't believe anyone who tries to tell you that one of the written commandments about traveling is that you must sleep and cook outdoors. It isn't true. I looked at the bed with a kind of fondness prompted by too close an association with pine needles, dirt, nylon, exposed branches, cold drafts, and gypsy bears. Besides, nothing is written.

But that night turned out neither to be comfortable nor comforting. I slipped into bed about ten. Lying awake, I stared at the ceiling and remembered how Thomas Moran (the painter) used to create, late in life, interesting landscapes from the cracks in his ceiling plaster. The light by the bed threw distorted shadows over the room, but exposed the ceiling above me. After looking at its wrinkled, medieval surface with its web of cracks, I decided not to make gardens from wildernesses or daisies from thornbushes.

Sleep came, a cool smooth sleep. But at eleven I fell or moved to the center of the bed and a wayward spring poked my back. I turned over, but eventually the strange centrifugal force of ancient beds pulled me back to the center. Again I returned to the edge, but natural law soon prevailed.

Beds, like bowling shoes, have seen myriad personalities. Usually a good bed, like a good shoe, is hard to find. They save the best beds for the penthouse suites at the Hilton. All others are sent to clearinghouses where they are shipped to towns under

300,000 population. If a good one arrives inadvertently, it is purloined by the motel manager for his own, or sent packing.

All the worst beds are saved for those jaded travelers who check in after seven at night and interrupt the manager's viewing of the third rerun of "*Leave it to Beaver.*" I've seen this treatment firsthand. Usually, if you ask for a single at eight at night, the manager will stumble in barefooted, grow momentarily silent, rub his chin reflectively, and pretend to think of available, maidscoured rooms. In truth he is counting the number of bumps and bruises and scrapes in the mattress of number seventeen, as punishment for interrupting the Beav's and Wally's chess match.

I dropped off about eleven thirty again, the bed and I in a cold war of mutual dislike. Sleep returned, a cottony sleep that contrasted with the furious slumber around Mount Sneffels the night before. I lay in the deep hollow of the bed's middle, which is the instant mark that it is loved and revered by legions of travelers.

At one in the morning the bed shook. The window rattled. I heard swelling in the night outside the most resonant howl—not just the howl of a dog, but a cavernous, full-throated Baskerville hound howl that lunged into the dark.

I tramped to the window and looked out. Snow clung to the streets and steep cliffs; roofs angled up the sides of the mountains and a few pinpricks of light shone from under them. I thought I heard a human voice in the far distance, but I couldn't be sure. Briefly the howling stopped. I padded back to my adversary, rolled into the crisp sheets one more time, and clung to the salient edge of the bed.

At three the bellowing returned. At four again. I heard a muffled commotion in the adjacent room, fumbling on top of voices. A woman's voice rose and fell, and a man's voice punctuated the intervening silence. She was looking for something. At four in the morning she was, of all things, in need of a curling iron. There was a brief, muffled exchange of words, and then through my pillow I heard:

"Well, George, where could the damn thing be?"

"Shhhh!"

I counted the minutes till sunrise. I finally got up when the first feeble light hit the blinds, and I noticed that it was as quiet as the inside of a cloud. I left the bed for the last time, washed, and hurried out of the room, leaving behind forever a cracked ceiling, a misplaced curling iron, and the wild hound of Ouray.

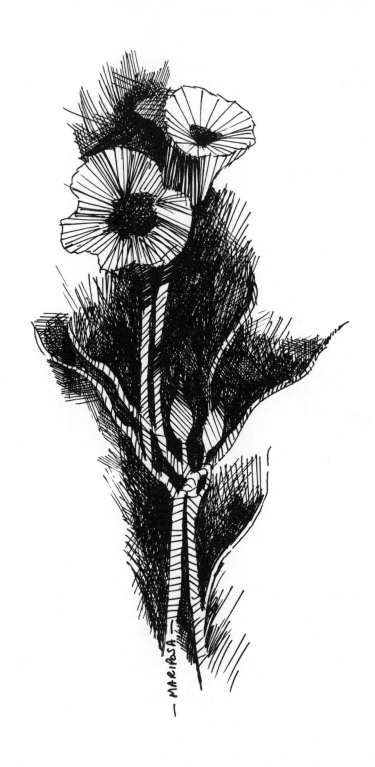

9

Marble

The first-time visitor to Colorado will soon discern that it is a unity of mountains and a diversity of plains, mesas, and basins. The drive north from the Uncompahgres descends into the fertile valleys of the Western Slope. Once more the mountains are abandoned, the road conforms to the riverbed of the Uncompahgre, and ascends, going east, at Delta.

Just above Delta at Read I turned the Jeep into one of the makeshift fruit stands that sprout like dandelions in late September and early October. The peaches this year were extraordinary.

"These yours?" I asked the woman behind the stand.

"Sure are."

"They *are* good."

"I know," she said. "One of the best crops in years. Some rain and a good mild sun. Where you headed?"

"Marble," I replied, after looking to the mountains.

"Marble? Ain't nobody in Marble. That place is deserted. Maybe except for a few hangers-on."

"I know. I thought I'd look at the quarries."

"Good, because there's plenty of them. A few shacks. Lots of marble, too. Used to go up there myself when I was a girl. Lotsa stone there."

I thanked her and took my fruit back to the Jeep. I shoved in the clutch, and with the knowledge that it was sound as new, I headed up into the mountains.

For many years the material that defined the classical world was marble.

Millions of years ago, the limestone in this area underwent severe heating. Molten rock intruded into overlying rock layers. The limestone recrystalized, literally changed identities, to form the hard marble deposits of the Marble area. This abrupt, inexorable warping and change of forms accompanied the dynamic shaping of the Colorado Rockies following the Mesozoic era. Other changes occurred—shales became slates, sandstones became quartzites.

This shaping and heating (especially heating, because it destroyed the organic matter that could turn the limestone black) reorganized the crystals of the rock, and produced the pure white marble of Yule Creek, near Marble. But it was the ancients who began to recognize marble as a reflection of the perfection of the visible world.

To the Egyptians, marble was a rare commodity. But for them the material was not as important as the idea being represented. In other words, a figure could be carved in slate, diorite, or gold, according to position and rank, but the primary purpose of art was to instruct. Pharoahs, of course, would be represented in the most elegant material available, but sometimes even these materials seem crude considering the status of the king.

The Greeks, who worshiped perfection in art, were really the first people to give marble consistent recognition. The hills, plains, and cities of Greece are littered with the reminders of their love of *arete*. The medium became as important as the idea. Consequently, the temples of the Acropolis are an outgrowth of the Greek's vision of man, marble, and perfection.

To the Greek's, man's bodily proportion was the measuring scale of the universe. How the length of the arm related to the length of the leg determined the relationship in architecture from one column to the next. The building was the direct reflection of the man. In this way, from man to building to universe, there was a revelation of perfection, geometry, and reason.

The perfect world. How that has a way of dying on our

tongues—it seems a futile possibility for our age. But for centuries perfection in art was achieved through the use of marble in
sculpture and architecture.

The great sculptors of the Classical Age, Phidias and later Prax-
iteles, experienced the true love of marble's capacities. No material, ancient or modern, achieves the surface luster or represents
the transparency and warmth of flesh as well as marble.

And so through the classical world, down through Athens,
Pergamum, and Rome, marble expressed the majesty, grace,
simplicity, and range of human perfection. Of course, the architecture of Rome was borrowed from the Greeks. The Roman
forums and decaying villas were in the classical style, but Greek
in intuition and conception.

The Romans loved marble because it asserted power and elegance. The tall Corinthian column in Roman architecture simply
extended the limits of the simple Greek Doric column. When
the Romans, in the midst of building an empire, turned from
perfect architecture to practical, from temples to roads, bridges,
and aqueducts, the love of marble as an expressive medium began to wane and die.

The stony roads leading to Rome are a statement about the
death of classicism: the love of perfection could only be handled
on a small scale. Once architecture and sculpture could be mass
produced, the need for perfection was abandoned.

After the collapse of Rome, the monuments that were scat-
tered over Europe were made of the local stone of Chartres,
Rheims, and Salisbury. The Age of Faith had no need of the sublime materials of Greece and Rome. The gray granite of sculpture
produced a surface roughness that veiled the figure, indeed
bundled up the body, that the Greeks had left nude.

But with the Renaissance a new spirit emerged which re-
kindled the love of man, perfection, architecture, mathematics,
and marble. The new men of the age—Michelangelo, Bramante,
Raphael, and later Bernini—championed a return to the classical
world by resurrecting its materials. Marble, the flesh of Hermes
to the Greeks, was used for the new proud tower of Europe, Saint
Peter's Basilica. Inspired by the *Bible*, Michelangelo chiseled a
heroic and tempestuous conception of Moses.

By the sixteenth century the Carrara marble quarries in Italy
hummed with activity. Tons of marble were cut and hauled into

artist's studios. A new age had discovered marble's expressive capabilities.

Marble was the stone of aristocratic Europe, particularly when it wanted to honor the classical world. By 1800 a so-called Greek revival style had emerged that captured both the material and the spirit. It was apparent by now that the modern nations of Europe wished to glorify, if not steal, some of the classical virtues of harmony, grace, and perfection. Buildings in this revival style sprouted up all over Europe and America, announcing an allegiance between the democracy of Greece and the rising egalitarian nations in America and Europe.

But that was it. Something was beginning to change toward the end of the nineteenth century and into the twentieth. That change would make Marble, Colorado, briefly soar with opportunity and then, without warning, make it plummet in a slow, winding economic spiral.

In July 1890 the first organized attempt was made to establish a quarry in Yule Creek, near Marble. Even by then experts had graded the marble equal to the stone from the Vermont and Carrara quarries. Marble was on its way to establishing itself as the West's leading exporter of the great classical medium.

But the art world was silently conspiring against the windfall at Marble and Carrara, and against the spirit of classicism in general. For centuries, classical art was the epitome of the rationality of the Western world. But by 1900, artists turned away from the materials of perfection and sought those that mirrored the imperfection and disorder of twentieth-century culture: wood, tin, wire, bronze, and plastics. The need for marble in sculpture was gradually abandoned.

In architecture, a rising middle class demanded a utilitarian style. Although classical styles were still popular, they were being limited to shrines and state offices. Marble, Colorado, received the commission to quarry the stone for the Lincoln Memorial and the Washington Monument at a time when the economy of the city went into a tailspin. The modern world demanded practicality and material strength from its architecture. So the new functional order replaced marble with steel. The soaring office complex had replaced the temple; the spiral parking garage had overshadowed the villa and the forum.

In 1917 the population of Marble was 1,400; in 1926, 600; in 1932, 225. As the gradual wane of the classical style took hold, the economy of the city collapsed. The great steel and glass cages of the modern city had at last silenced the voice and spirit of the classical style.

Now the ruins of the Yule Creek quarries are as white and empty as the fallen stones of Delphi. Even under the snow there is an eerie resemblance to the cities of antiquity, a certain silence that falls upon the hills and preserves the memory of its former tenants. If it weren't for the thick aspen and the huge chalk hills, you would think that you had been dropped into Herculaneum or Troy.

Just north on the highway I turned into the Redstone Inn. How conspicuous it looks with its mixed Dutch and Tudor exterior, standing in broad lawns against the belts of aspen, pine, and fir.

Actually the accommodations were a model of early twentieth-century efficiency and cleanliness. Founded in 1902 by John Osgood, Redstone was a mining village with one important distinction: the miners were housed in cottages and not in the lice-infested shacks usually accorded laborers in mining camps.

Osgood was aware of the effects of close urbanization of workers. The rows of tenements and row houses in the English Midlands were testament to the horrors of factory life in the nineteenth century.

This was Osgood's grand experiment, to provide clean domestic quarters to workers who had toiled all day in the mines. About seventy small homes were included in the original plan, plus a firehouse and a central clubhouse. The Redstone Inn, the largest of the buildings, was reserved for bachelors.

In the end Osgood's vision was successful; the village was and is a unique social environment in an era known for the exploitation of and indifference toward miners and working gangs in general.

I had descended from the classical world of Marble into the Victorian world of Redstone Inn. I had passed from the tossed and broken marble slabs along the Crystal River to the clean edges and roofs of Redstone. And nothing replaces the classical silence of broken, ancient stone like solid Victorian propriety.

The lawns of Redstone are thick and trim as Armstrong carpets, and the porcelain in the dining room shines in the cool northern light. The curtains are starched and lure the soft discs of sunlight. Waitresses swirl like butterflies, alight, and disappear with your order. The kitchen looks capable of serving Peking duck or a good hamburger. People smile, forks kiss plates, chairs only rustle on the floor, men and women whisper like they are in love. Everything works like Newton's universe: mechanical, ordered, punctual. I am grateful.

I devoured a sizzling steak while looking out the window at the lawns and sunshine. I paid the bill and walked out into the parking lot. The dry mild weather still conspired against the advancing season. The sun, the feeble wind, the ultramarine sky with one cloud pinned to it—combined and attacked the senses like one massive inoculation against the onset of winter's dreariness.

There was a strip of lawn close to the parking lot , and I noticed two young cyclists breaking out their picnic lunches. By now the shadows fell limply across the grass, covering their gear, their black and red shorts, and their Raleigh racers, shiny even in the evergreen shadow. I guessed they had just pulled off the road for a quick bite to eat.

They were both from Denver University and were on their way to Grand Junction for a race. They had chugged up Vail Pass, muscled it into Glenwood's gurgling springs, and turned south, for a lark, to visit Redstone and follow a fork of the Gunnison River. The girl, her hair tied softly into her bike helmet, looked fresher than her male friend. He looked at me with a weary eye— a kind of quick summation of the whole exhausting trip.

They nibbled on that lunch that I've seen people eat before they assault Everest. Looking at them in their own separate stages of exhaustion, I couldn't imagine how anyone could criss-cross Colorado on a bike and enjoy it.

At sea level the bike is an instrument of God and angels. But at 8,000, 9,000, and 10,000 feet it turns quickly into a vehicle of torture and humiliation. Even on minor passes, the lungs plead for oxygen and receive only meager amounts of thin air; thighs and calves balloon and tighten; torsos undergo a persistent bludgeoning, like steel fists against the kidneys. And then when the rider reaches the summit, he may face, not his reward, but further punishment. The sun that had blinded the rider for miles and percolated his weary blood, now disappears into clouds. Convectional rain drenches his body and soul. The temperature plunges from seventy to forty-five in minutes. The body that seemed like a furnace fights off the chills, the demons of exhaustion, and the forests of dizziness. Hypothermia can kill him if the mountains do not.

But I did not mention anything about sweat, legs, lungs, or rain. Somehow the surroundings didn't warrant it.

"This must be the best weather to ride in," I said.

"It's ideal," said the girl. "It's the drivers that are the worst part of the trip. That's one of the reasons we turned off the highway at Glenwood—the crazies are out on the road."

"What do they do?"

"Everything—from trying to run you off the pavement to throwing pop cans at you—you name it, they try it."

I sat down in the chill grass. I remembered for a moment the other delights of cycling in the mountains. I said: "What makes it worthwhile?"

The girl looked at her boyfriend and tried to weigh his expression. She did not speak for a moment. Then she laughed. "The freedom. It sounds so silly after you think about everything. But there is nothing like the sense of being apart from everything, and yet being caught up in something very large."

There is in every motorist a cyclist yearning to break loose. For a moment I almost envied them. The urge crossed me—very fleetingly—to barter the Jeep for the Raleighs. I thought momentarily of the oneness with the trees and air that the girl talked about, but that quickly dissolved into visions of aching legs and unexpected cloudbursts.

I pushed the Jeep up the open road, hoping that I would see them one day as part of a race in Durango, Denver, or Boulder. They would be part of that swaying phalanx of riders, brightly colored, a flickering collection of knees, bowed heads, and elbows flying by. And in spite of the downpours, the aching sides, the spent legs, the hurled beer cans, the weary lungs, they would be part of the wind. They would know the provinces of the reckless animal soul and feel the throb of its wild heartbeat.

And I just might go with them.

10

Maroon Bells

October 5:

When you wander into the Maroon Bells Valley you realize why humans have carried on a sustained love affair with mountains. I suppose it has a lot to do with the concept of beauty, that proper combination of terror, fear, and awe that so inspired the poets and painters of the nineteenth century.

But our affair with mountains has been a short one. Nature, of course, has been at the center of our thinking since antiquity. It has always served as a metaphor for conduct, reasoning, and morality. But the idea that you should acknowledge, let alone love, mountains is relatively new in our experience.

In Europe mountains were first thought of as unnecessary barriers to communication and transportation, and then only ruffians and religious hermits bothered hiding out in their shadows. They hardly appear in art until the sixteenth century, when Pieter Brueghel the Elder did some vigorous and insightful sketches of the Alps. Leonardo da Vinci, too, seemed genuinely moved by the Alps, for his sketches of them reveal his interests in the organic vitality of the plants and animals of the high, craggy slopes.

Before the eighteenth century, traveling to see a mountain, or indeed climbing one, would have seemed perfectly ludicrous to most rational people. But around the year 1340, Petrarch, the Italian poet, decided to assault Mount Ventoux. He made it to the top and was stimulated by the surrounding vistas. He ended up, though, being humbled by a line from Saint Augustine's *Confessions*, which he unfortunately brought with him to the summit. Petrarch read that "nothing counts except the soul." The admonishment amid such visual beauty must have been too much for him—he never climbed a mountain again, and neither did most people for a long time afterward.

But in the late eighteenth century mountains became stimulating, as you can tell by the torrent of poetry written about them. And by the time of Lord Byron and Percy Shelley, mountains assumed a near religious connotation. So for this new group of poets and artists mountains became the loftiest symbols of the sublime, and perhaps represented, as John Ruskin believed, the liberation of the soul.

In painting, mountains inspired two artists of note, J. M. W. Turner and Caspar Friedrich, who were both European in training and outlook. For Turner, who was volatile by nature, mountains expressed the furious aspects of natural elements. He saw the vast, sheer Alpine slopes as victims of snowstorms, thunderstorms, and violent lightning storms. Friedrich saw the mountains as powerful creations that dwarfed humans and their aspirations. There is loneliness in Friedrich's mountains; there is raw energy in Turner's.

For American artists, who inherited this worship of the sublimity of mountains, and who were reared near the White Mountains, the Adirondacks, and the Berkshires, the high peaks became the available symbols of the natural and remote beauty of the eastern United States. But when the painters came to the Rockies, the mountains assumed a grandeur unmatched by the hills of the East. Albert Bierstadt and Thomas Moran, both foreign-born Americans, traversed the West and the Rockies in search of the kind of pictorial stimulation that Turner and Friedrich had sought in the Alps.

The Rocky Mountains begged to be idealized, and Moran and Bierstadt quickly obliged. Their paintings are glowing conceptions of the vastness of the Rockies. Bierstadt came first in 1859 and zigzagged up and down the Front Range, finally pushing into the summits beyond Idaho Springs. Moran came to the Rockies in the early 1870s, was smitten with their dynamic colors, and kept coming back periodically after that. There is hardly a breath of wind in Bierstadt's mountains; everywhere there is

grandeur dominated by the palest, unearthly summits. For Moran, who was infected with a similar idealism, the granite of
mountains and cliffs became marble, and the most powdery
limestone became alabaster. For both artists, the great canyons
were seen as cathedrals and the mountains as the shining temples of myth.

I parked the Jeep and took to the path that twists around Maroon Creek, sensing how Moran had fallen victim to this gauntlet
of color. Drifts of snow still lingered in patches, but the tawny
ground of autumn still prevailed. In this valley the stands of
aspen still remind you that they are second in importance only to
the peaks. But even now their yellow leaves had turned slightly
brown, become paper webs of decay, waiting for the wind to
scatter them along the spine of Colorado.

The poetry of autumn in the mountains is silence. The path to
Maroon Peak is as crowded as Lourdes in summer. But in fall the
quietness becomes an inevitable part of the journey, as it speaks
or murmurs in subtle ways. The aspen are quiet, the sky is quiet,
and the brooks roar with trickles.

The sky was as blue as lapis. People, of course, boast of their
cities and the skies above them, and I won't challenge them. But
at this altitude and robbed of its moisture, the Colorado sky has
the purest intensity and the most startling sense of tangibility.
When the bright yellow aspen leaves are seen against it, the contrast is brutally beautiful.

Nothing in nature rivals the competition of these colors. Even
Van Gogh's landscape paintings of Arles diminish in purity of
color next to the spellbinding blues, oranges, and yellows of
these mountains.

Particularly in autumn is the intensity at its limit. Then the
clouds have moved on, the sun burns in an empty cobalt sky, and
the air is dry but warm.

I made the hike to Maroon Lake and back in about two hours.
The path is civilized. For artists, the composition of descending
mountain lines, vertical trees, and the graceful Maroon Peaks is
unmatched in the Rockies.

Down the road is Aspen, originally created by the silver boom
in the late nineteenth century. It is now known for its culture, its

snow, and its architecture, which is a forest of doll-sized Victorian and Gothic dwellings with a surprising amount of domestic charm.

The road from Aspen to Independence Pass contains a series of long switchbacks relieved by broad belts of aspen. At the top of the pass, which is over 12,000 feet high, I parked the Jeep and tried to take in the overwhelming sweep of bald mountain peaks.

Of course, Colorado is a network of these passes, some of awesome stature, such as this one, and others at 9,000 feet are mere rises in the road. There names are as various and wild—Rabbit Ears, Wolf Creek, Lizard Head, Muddy, Kenosha, Slumgullion, La Manga—and somehow descriptive of their uniqueness. For Colorado writer Frank Waters, the passes were both kind and cruel; particularly the caprices of nature played havoc in these partings of the rock.

The Motorist's Tale

They are all incomparable and unpredictable; they span lofty horizons to link the old with new; and they span as well some of the most spectacular space on the continent. Through these defiles, first worn into ancient game trails by hoof and claw, have passed the fabulous parade of Indians, mountain men, twenty mule team freighters, crack trains and boiling Fords that in one century have telescoped our entire history. . . .

A stranger, helplessly dominated by space and mass or merely entranced by the view, will stare at the glistening, jagged peaks. But a native's glance forever ranges uneasily back and forth along the rim hunting for the notch that will let him through or over the wall. Gunsight Pass. It is a generic name for that feature of the landscape as ever-present in fact as in pulp-paper westerns, and there are few which have not been so known locally despite their other names. . . .

I remember being stopped one late afternoon in a little town at the foot of a pass in Colorado. A chain was stretched across the road and a long queue of cars was being turned back by the town constable. "Snow on the pass," he said. True, there had been a light spring flurry, the clouds still hung

low over the ridges. But the lilacs were out, the wind was
warm, and the pass was barely 9,000 feet high. Besides, this
was May 7th. Imagine mere weather refuting the calendar in
1936! Good-naturedly we all turned back for an hour or two
until the mistake should be rectified.

Instead, it got worse. The wind developed voice and
temper. The clouds dropped like a blanket fallen off the closet
shelf, and fresh snowflakes fluttered out like moths. Mean-
while more and more cars had driven in until the narrow
street was jammed.

It was suddenly dark. Angry salesman in light spring suits,
stalled motorists, frightened tourists and perplexed campers
made a dash to the hotel. Wives and husbands separated to
crowd three or four to a room; cots were placed in the halls.
When the hotel was full, citizens offered spare rooms and par-
lor sofas. By eight o'clock every cafe and lunch counter was
out of fresh food. The proprietor simply waved cheerfully at
the cans on the shelf. "Point her out, mister. We'll open and
warm her up."

. . . By midnight, drawn together in the solidartiy of those
who are called to share an unexpected and novel experience,
we settled for the night. Fat businessmen wrapped themselves
in overcoats on the lobby floor. A flour salesman passed
round his bottle. Lights were snapped off. The fire died.

Yet no one slept. Upstairs a frightened child could not be
hushed. Somewhere, in the church belfry perhaps, a loose bell
was whipping back and forth, tolling faintly but wildly. Above
all this rose the shrieks of the wind. Two state highway patrolmen came in, covered with snow, and tried to telephone.
The line was dead. "What's up, officer? How long are we
stuck?" asked a sleepy voice. There was no answer. As they
went out, admitting a blast of cold wind, we caught in the
glimmer of street lights a glimpse of icy pavement and whirl-
ing sleet.

Stark, unreasonable fear rose. What had happened? A snow-
storm had blocked the road over the hill for a single night. It
was more than that. It was as if the hairline balance of man's
dominance over nature, achieved after centuries of struggle,
had suddenly been lost and we were again at the mercy of

those elements we had ignored so long and comfortably. Our thoughtless assumptions of security had been destroyed. The smooth course of our lives had been rudely checked.

In that small mountain town, high on the breast of a wild and lawless continent, we were as helpless, lost and frightened as passengers on a stricken ocean liner—and that loose bell, pealing wildly through the dark canyons and overhanging cliffs, carried the same tone of frantic futility. With its endless, unanswered ring in our ears we awaited dawn and then rushed to doors and windows.

Before us at the end of the block rose a great wall of Colorado mountains, two thousand feet high. It was white with snow. What we could see of the entrance to the pass was an unbroken drift. Branches of trees littered the icy street. Cloth tops of cars were shredded canvas. The silence was suddenly broken. Three women rushing for the hall bathroom upstairs had got into a wrangle.

All morning a crowd of people thrown out of joint milled in the street. Townspeople, so hospitable the night before, were curt at answering questions. The price of tire chains doubled. The stark, unreasonable fear of night was replaced by a surly, unreasonable anger—at what no one knew. They only felt the immense snowy wall of indomitable rock press in upon the flimsy brick and shingle, upon minds and nerves.

At noon escape was offered. A road back across the plain was cleared; people were advised to take the long detour. But no one budged. American stubbornness set in. Humanity in its ceaseless struggle with nature cannot give in anywhere.

At last, near four o'clock, a single funereal line of cars struck up over the hill. The first two promptly slid off into a ditch and heeled over with broken axles. Damned by road crews, blocked by the snowplow, the rest of us reached the summit in low gear after five hours. Here we were forced to wait two more while another file followed up a second plow from the other side. There was no room to pass; the drifts on each side were higher than the tops of the stalled cars.

By the time state highway patrolmen finally took hold, it was after midnight and bitterly cold. Fires were lit, and between these we snaked downward yards at a time with sleepless eyes and numbed hands and feet. And when at last we finally got down the pass in wan daylight, it was only to find the level highway still partially obstructed by fallen telephone poles and tangled wires.

Such may be the annoying hazards of a modern pass for travelers. But without these open passes, the mountain walls close like the jaws of a trap. A whole people may be caught and held in helpless imprisonment.

Lady's Slipper

11

Leadville

October 6:

Both in a geographical and historical sense, Leadville is the heart
of the Colorado mountains. It has one of the highest mineral
concentrations in the world, supplying quantities of gold, silver,
manganese, and lead. When gold was discovered here in 1860
the boom began. From then until 1881 a strident sense of
prosperity overtook Leadville. It developed a fairly sophisticated
society, encouraged the arts, and briefly saw to it that culture and
mining could mingle peacefully.

To Horace Tabor, originally from Vermont, Leadville seemed
the perfect place for an opera house. He had spent his youth
struck with gold fever, first in the Pikes Peak rush of 1859 and
then wandering from stake to stake throughout Colorado. He
finally settled in Leadville, gambled his meager fortune on the
mines, and within a few years built up his assets beyond
$9,000,000. By 1879 Leadville was a hodgepodge of beer halls,
literary societies, theaters, and social clubs.

"Tabor wanted to add to the pile," remarked the bartender
over the din of the seven o'clock crowd. I sat listening over the
bar on which everyone in Leadville in the last fifty years had cut
their immortal signatures. "So Tabor built the biggest, fanciest
place this side of the Mississippi. Called it 'the temple of amuse-
ment.' Opening night was in 1879, and attendance was down

because two days before the vigilantes hanged two men in the city jail. Tabor was furious that his evening was ruined by the bad publicity."

"But the Opera House was a success?"

"Tremendously. From then on the great names of the theater stopped here: Laurence Barrett, Helena Modjeska—."

"Oscar Wilde?"

"Oh, yes, *and* Oscar Wilde."

It was a weary Oscar Wilde who peered out at the shacks and splendors of Leadville from the island of his train seat. He saw no one to greet him, so when the train had stopped, he grabbed his cane, and left his carriage for the cold air of the platform.

He looked up and down the rails, and after ascertaining no welcoming committee would be arriving, asked directions to the Clarendon Hotel.

He strolled in his customary tweeds toward the hotel and entered through the ladies' entrance. Once ensconced in his rooms and having survived a hot bath, he received the shuffling lines of curious townspeople.

He stretched out his six-foot figure on a resplendent sofa, pulled his shoulder-length hair over his ears and prepared to do battle. He wheezed at last (the altitude was taking its toll) and took several abrupt gulps of air.

Several people familiar with his book of *Poems* and eccentric reputation filed through, gawking at and sizing up the creature they believed came from either Wonderland or the Antipodes. They could not be sure which. They shuffled in, their heavy boots scarring the immaculate floor which had been specially prepared for Wilde's visit. Wilde noticed them too, though he seemed preoccupied with the shininess of his fingernails. Their faces—lean, pretty, soiled, inquisitive, desperate, sneering—flashed before him, as they filed in and ambled out.

That night, Wilde ate and dressed in the comfort of his rooms, then prepared his lecture on the *Ethics of Art.* He wrote the manuscript in an elegant longhand, inserting some illuminating passages from the autobiography of Benvenuto Cellini. If these were miners, he reasoned, then it was his responsibility to educate them in the criticism of art.

Into the Tabor Opera House Wilde strutted dressed in black

velvet, a wide Byron collar, low shoes, and black stockings. His
hair now was neatly combed and parted in the middle, though it
danced on his shoulders as he walked to the lectern. He pro-
ceeded right to his speech without any introduction from his
sponsors.

He spread out the pages before him. The top of the first page
was neatly titled: "The Practical Application of the Aesthetic
Theory to Exterior and Interior House Decoration, with Observa-
tions on Dress and Personal Ornament."

He kept his pitch at about middle C, and for about an hour
discussed beauty and art. The audience listened patiently, seemingly uncomfortable with the subjects, but riveted on Wilde's
pedantic presentation.

Several days later, after having stirred up controversy in town
by his outrageous dress, Wilde was asked to tour Horace Tabor's
Matchless Mine.

Wilde descended into the dripping earth in a crushed iron
bucket in which it "was impossible to be graceful." Wilde and his
party were met at the bottom by a dozen miners, each bearing a
bottle of bourbon. The Western custom was to have every bottle
make the rounds, so Wilde, bowing to convictions, took twelve
snorts and proclaimed to the miners that they were all "very
charming."

He told Bill Bush, Tabor's associate, on the way back to the
Clarendon that these lads in Leadville (or as Wilde heard it acidly
referred to as Deadville) were "not at all rough and were an
excellent audience."

I left the bar and stopped near the the Tabor Opera House. It
had begun to snow, not the belligerent snow of Ouray, but
the soft furtive kind when cats turn once and lie peacefully in the
rounds of pillows till morning. I walked back to the hotel. The
wind had dropped completely so that the voices of the night
were husky, frosty, and near.

Just north of Leadville, but well off the road, is the Mount of
the Holy Cross, made famous by William H. Jackson's photograph of 1873. I arrived there the next morning under a wide
blue sky.

In summer the residual snows form a near perfect cruciform.

With a shaft nearly 1,500 feet long, the mountain has long been a landmark. Jackson's photograph inspired the English-born painter Moran to make the arduous pilgrimage up the Arkansas River to behold the sacred sight.

Moran was a gifted but not too original artist who designed his spectacular vistas under vaporous skies borrowed from his god, J. M. W. Turner. He usually included the required amount of waterfalls, dark canyons, and shimmering backdrops to scintillate even the minor admirer of nature. If he was limited as an original painter, however, he was a superb colorist who turned the canyons, mesas, and summits of Colorado into spectacular cinemas of color and dissolving light.

A lover of the panoramas of Yellowstone,* Moran was driven to see and paint the Mount of the Holy Cross. In 1874 Moran and a climbing party set out from a camp on the Arkansas. After a strenuous ascent through intervening mountains, passes, and swamps, they crossed the Continental Divide through Tennessee Pass and then reached the valley below Notch Mountain. The following morning the group began the final climb which would bring them in view of the peak. At two thirty that afternoon, still eight hundred feet from their intended viewpoint of the mount, Moran and his party collapsed from exhaustion. But he could see the mountain and the cross: "We rested half an hour and then started on the back track, getting back to camp in three hours. In the valley is one of the most picturesque waterfalls . . . I shall use it in the foreground of my picture."

I suspect that Moran felt cheated at not having the spectacular view of the mount that was afforded Jackson. Moran's depiction of the peak in his huge painting *The Mount of the Holy Cross, Colorado* is based on Jackson's photograph and not on his own sketches. As Moran had planned, the landforms in the painting were conveniently reassembled: the waterfall that normally cannot be seen against the mountains now glides furiously in the painting under the trees, slopes, and formidable Mount of the Holy Cross itself. Moran simply made nature's imperfections a little more acceptable. In this case Moran's blood knew that a

* Indeed, his painting *Grand Canyon of the Yellowstone* of 1871 inspired Congress to make Yellowstone a national park. "Yellowstone" Moran went on to sanctify other prominent landmarks of the Rockies through his art.

dynamic painting of the mount would have to bring together a
pastiche of details. The blood was right.

Moran sent his finished work, a seven-by-six-foot canvas, off to the Centennial Exposition of 1876, where it was awarded a medal and diploma. When the painting was exhibited at the Royal Academy in England, Mrs. William Bell of Colorado Springs acquired it after three months of negotiations with Moran.

For many years the painting hung in Briarhurst, the Bell home in Manitou Springs, Colorado. In January 1886, a fatal fire broke out at the Bell's home. Mrs. Bell shepherded the family outdoors, darted back in, and with the help of the butler, cut Moran's canvas from the securely fastened frame and took it to safety.

Mrs. Bell's husband retired in 1905, and the family moved the painting to England. *The Mount of the Holy Cross, Colorado,* Thomas Moran's cinematic tribute to the Colorado Rockies, hung in Bell's estate, Pendell Court, Surrey, England, for a number of years before it was purchased by a New York museum.

12

Two Artists, Two Cities

U.S. ROUTE 70
October 8:

There are two things that link me to Vail, art and skiing. I know
something about the former and the latter is becoming easier,
but its mastery will always be elusive. There is a tidiness, a brisk
internationalism, and an alpine domesticity to Vail. It is one of
the youngest of the brood of major ski areas, located in a little
bowl off the interstate with the enormous Gore Range mountains looming over it.

I resigned to spend a few days here. The drive had been steady
for the last week, and I was seeking a sanctuary of sorts.

The weather had warmed when I arrived. The snow was melting in the streets and only bare traces of it ribboned the mountains. I swung the Jeep up behind the city, about a mile above
Gore Creek and pulled into the driveway of a medium-sized
A-frame.

It was Larry Darnell's house—an artist and good friend. Someone who takes art seriously is always dangerous to be around
and such is Larry. He abandoned New York for these mountains
and has maintained an endless pilgrimage up here ever since.

We met on the spacious deck that overlooked the great belts
of evergreen sprawling around the town. He had not changed
much, and upon going inside and viewing his paintings on their
easels, I found that neither had his art.

There is no other way to describe Larry's art than magical, mysterious, provocative, and never realistic. He cultivates the primitive and the symbolic. He eschews trends, although he does admit to traditional values in art.

I examined a particular canvas with a series of very bold but crude abstract images.

"Shouldn't primitive art be left for the past?" I asked, a little sarcastically, I'm afraid.

"Perhaps just the opposite," he replied with a slight smile. "The more we become modern, the more we remove ourselves from the impulses which produced our spirits."

"And technology. Is that a modern evil?"

"I suppose a limited amount of technology is good. I mean I like to plug in the coffee pot as much as the next person. But there is a sane level of progress—and I think it's the person's responsibility to stop buying when it isn't necessary."

"Not the company's?" I responded.

"The company will always go on producing and inventing. We the consumer must stop it in the kitchen and the living room."

"But, Larry, aren't you placing enormous responsibility on the consumer?"

"Yes, but with all of our freedom a little prudent responsibility ten minutes a day isn't asking much, is it?"

I shrugged it off and we sat down. Larry poured me a cup of coffee, and we exchanged some words. I told him about the trip and basically what I was up to.

"Discovered anything yet?" he asked.

"Yes, a good deal. Probably far more than I can think about right now. I suppose when I get back and write it up things will begin to make sense."

That afternoon after unpacking a few things, I strolled into Larry's living room/studio and noticed him in the grips of his art. The painting was composed of bright colors in crude simple forms. Larry attacked the canvas as if in a trance; I could see the concentration welling up through his brain and into his eyes.

"Do you understand the Indian artist's mentality?" He asked at last.

"I've just come from Mesa Verde—their art is everywhere. And yes, I think I understand it."

"Well, you might say I try for a type of magic through certain

symbols. A mountain in my art becomes a flat abstract shape of a
pyramid."

"Why?"

"Because the pyramid is more than just the shape—the history, the whole baggage of mysticism and magic are contained in that one symbol. The mountain, any mountain, has a general sameness that is uninteresting and powerless."

"Do you think the Egyptians knew of the power of that shape?"

"I'm convinced." said Larry. "When I was in Cairo I was even more sure that the pyramid form was known to the ancients in a far more complex way than we can even begin to understand. And great power is transmitted through such simple shapes."

"Cézanne's sphere, cone, and cylinder,* you mean?"

"Yes, but not totally. Cézanne speaks of nature. I'm also talking about magic and mystery."

"I must say you've lost me."

"Sorry, but to me the shape or symbol must have magical possibilities—such as the pyramids at Giza—powerful, magical images. Another one is the Roman arch. Sound strange? Well it is half a circle, so it would qualify with Cézanne. But think of it. That half circle has a connotation of five hundred years of misery, transportation, armies, empires, and the whole commerce of Rome tied to it. As a symbol it is much more expressive than all of Gibbon."

"But doesn't the viewer have to recognize the symbol in order for it to have meaning? Not everyone knows a Roman arch from a Latin cross. Or a Greek temple from the pyramids."

"Not everyone, of course" Larry responded. "But the very reason that these are symbols is because of their universality. And people, depending on their various backgrounds and levels of intelligence, bring fewer or greater meanings to the symbol. The symbol, of course, is as rich as you can make it, or wish to make it."

"So the primitive, abstract shape is part of the psychological language of mankind?"

---

* One of the pioneers of modern art, Cézanne maintained that nature is composed of these basic shapes.

"Yes. And have you noticed another shape common to a lot of primitive cultures worldwide?"

Larry walked over to the studio table. He squeezed a tube of red paint onto the palette and then rubbed his right hand into it. He held it up for me to see. He then crossed the room, looked at all the shapes in his painting and placed his scarlet hand squarely in the right-hand corner. He smiled.

"At Tulum in Mexico, Lascaux in France, and Mesa Verde, Colorado—and now Vail—the most expressive, generic, and magical signature of man has again been rendered."

"Is that the bond you share with other cultures?" I asked.

"Yes, but I think it's more than a bond. It shows recognition and renewal. Besides, I'll never forget seeing all those handprints in the caves of France or the temples of Yucatan. They scrambled up sometimes on each other's shoulders to make those prints, on lintels, rocks, or cave walls. The whole record of human struggle is in those handprints."

It seemed to me that Larry had discovered something at this point in his life—something that makes the heart peaceful and keeps stars burning.

The next two days we spent talking, lounging on the deck, and going for long walks around Vail. On the third day it was time to leave. I said good-bye to Larry. As I drove west out of Vail, I thought of Larry's strong, colorful paintings, the particular cliffs we teeter on, and the separate paths we pound to the truth.

The land drops again out of Vail, and the road turns north into the Yampa Valley. Amid ranches strewn up the hills and around streams, the cliffs are torn with coal mines and split by railroad tracks which thread the tenuous entrance into the source of the Yampa River. At the valley's northern boundary with Routt National Forest is Steamboat Springs.

Steamboat is the most northern oasis of the great ski areas of Colorado. Unlike Vail, it has a homesteaded appearance, and a pragmatic, earthy main street. Around Steamboat some of the most expensive snow in the Rockies stretches up through the aspen of the big hills. Originally the springs here emitted a chugging sound, similar to a riverboat, and the town's name was born.

But the proper heritage of the West is not its tourism, its snow,

or its mines, but its wildlife and forests. I drove just north of
Steamboat and pulled into the driveway of a substantial cottage
backing on to the steep slopes of the national forest.

Like Larry, Ben Thompson tramped from the East Coast several years ago, embraced these mountains and this way of life, and set up a studio of sorts in his backyard. Ben's art captures in wood the wildlife of western Colorado, stressing the enormous elegance of the creatures of forest and sky.

At one point we were raving about the extraordinary fall weather, then the conversation shifted to sculpture.

Ben asked: "Have you ever wondered why there are so few great sculptors, say, after Bernini and Rodin?"

"I guess I hadn't. But you're right, come to think of it."

"I think it all has to do with math. There are more possibilities with painting and writing and music. Like architecture, sculpture has firm restrictions. This wood can be shaped in an infinite number of ways—but so *few* of the ways are beautiful. So great sculptors are few because innovation is near impossible."

"Is that why you returned to realism?" I asked.

"Yes, realism comforts me. Abstraction is discomforting."

I thought quickly of Larry's macabre, bold shapes. Then Ben went on.

"In art you should be truthful with your feelings. The essence, the spirit of animals can only be transmitted through realistic shapes."

The loveliest backyards contain not croquet sets, lawn chairs, beach balls, or dogs, but the instruments and creations of one's labor—half-finished sculpture; tossed wood models; chain saws; and erect, polished eagles, elk, and deer.

"What threatens your art?" I asked, surveying the beautiful debris of the yard.

"Ignorant people. People who live by the cruel delusion that the earth and wildlife should be subdued. That everything should come under man's domination, like Old Macdonald's Farm."

I walked over to a very large sculpture of a magnificent elk.

"Have you ever hunted?" I asked at last.

"Once when I was a boy in Pennsylvania, my father took me hunting. We got out into the field. I had a large shotgun. Then some grouse flew up. My father told me to shoot. I brought the rifle to my shoulder and hesitated. I waited too long. Shame filled me—mixed with feelings of cowardice and immaturity. And most of all I had let down my father. Now I look back at that incident as one of the most important moments of my life. Later I discovered art and sculpture. I found it is easier to destroy than it is to create—far easier—and that's why destruction is so prevalent and true creation so rare. Art healed all the old wounds and filled in all the gaps of my immature self."

"Do you still feel the same way about hunting?"

"Yes, but I do know the familiar reasons given in favor of it. I remind myself constantly of those reasons. But still, you can tell when something smells when everyone, or near everyone, uses the same excuse for doing it. People hunt because they like to kill; people use the excuse of controlling animal populations when, in fact, that is the furthest thing from their minds."

The following day I turned the Jeep around in Ben's front yard, waved to him disappearing down the driveway and headed south. I drove back through Steamboat, bearing left just south of town. I took the highway going east which throws you into the notorious fogs of Rabbit Ears Pass, where I would cross the Continental Divide for the fourth time on this trip.

There had been a light rain that morning, a steady drumming on the hood that persisted through my departure. I steadily gained altitude, up to 8,000 feet and gradually at 8,500 feet the ceiling and visibility started dropping. At 9,000 feet, an immense gray cloud immersed the Jeep and pushed itself into my headlights. Soon the visibility was no more than ten feet.

I heard a car whoosh by as I kept my speed to around fifteen to twenty miles an hour. The silence, except for the engine and the wheels, was deafening. Then I waited for the sound of more cars going in the opposite direction. There was a prolonged silence of five minutes, with no outside activity, just the steady repetition of white centerlines disappearing into my left headlight.

I couldn't see the side of the road, or I couldn't tell how sharply it fell away. I dropped the speed down to ten and kept going. I could tell I was still climbing slightly, though I didn't know how the top of the pass looked. Chances were that it widened, but I couldn't be sure.

Then I reached the top. The fog was as thick as honey, but the road widened. I dropped it into second. Suddenly and briefly, there was no visibility. I pulled to the right. The road started to descend and I could feel the tug forward.

I have read books about eighteenth-century sailors, who, when their ships were becalmed in a fog, would spend their mornings on deck with their hands cupped over their ears, listening for the slightest sound on the sea.

Well, there was a similar strain on my eyes and heart. For minutes there was no centerline and sometimes no road. About a mile past the summit, riding on the slimmest edge of existence, the fog broke. Almost immediately, the sun shone and the Jeep, for the first time in a half hour, enjoyed the pavement midway between the centerline and the shoulder of the road.

I have also read of those sailors, who, after breaking into the sun and a good wind, would deliriously throw parts of their cargo overboard. After surveying my spartan gear, I decided the mere relief would have to suffice, and let the Jeep coast down the long winding descent into the high prairie of Middle Park.

13

Up on The Roof

U.S. ROUTE 34
October 12:

I traversed Middle Park, the high valley split by the source of the Colorado River, and entered Rocky Mountain National Park at Grand Lake. I drove up to Phantom Valley, made camp, and for the first time in memory, slept under the enormous ceiling of stars.

The next morning after breakfast I took to the trailhead just north of camp and headed north to Thunder Pass. The day was warm, but the morning and late-afternoon coolness whispered of winter. Ahead of me an endless meadow dotted with evergreens stretched to the mountains.

I was alone. I was alone with all the tragic forces of nature around me, alone with death of the land and Shelley's wind with its "dirge of the dying year, to which this closing night will be the dome of a vast sepulcher." Or here, under a roof of ragged peaks and indolent sky, the trees nearly bare, still there was enough time to squeeze the season of its "last oozings hours by hours."

To walk is to give back to the earth the energy it has given you. That morning road confirmed for me that all the things which threaten to destroy us—nuclear war, conformity, feelings of despair and hopelessness—belong regrettably to the cities. The real resonance, to which we must commit, speaks through the rocks and trees and grasses, and once more through the harmonies of Pythagoras and the scales of Mozart. So it has been through the ancient world, and so it will be through this century, if we keep our ears to the earth.

Rocky Mountain National Park—four words that provoke a thousand pictures. The high alpine meadows surmounted by the furrowed roof of America and watered by meandering streams lure the artist, the naturalist, and the traveler. Bierstadt discovered the cinemascope painting here, finding the high vertical slopes contrasted to the dark green tree line and saffron meadows a perfect statement of nature's wildness, loveliness, and sheer size.

I kept a good pace toward Thunder Pass. I saw very few people; the meadows were as deserted as beaches after Labor Day. Most of the people I saw were burdened with backpacks, and weaving like yaks on slim footholds, they plodded up through the grass and trees. It was my second time in the park, but like calling on an old friend it required a fresh assessment of the relationship. I saw the lines of the trees a little differently; I heard the jays's and chickadee's arias with a more attentive ear; I perceived the colors with a surer sense of tone and hue. At three miles out I knew that I had new eyes. The park had not changed, except for growth here and there, but the vagabond heart had. It had grown, become wise in a way, experienced the love of the world, its art and history and culture, and now it was brought back to revolutionize this forest path.

Farther down the trail I met a man named Wilson, who under a spruce bough explained how he retreated to the park to avoid "the wife and daytime television." He lived in Loveland, just east of the Continental Divide.

He was perhaps in his early sixties and had a Merlin face, bushy moustache, and pointed beard that, when he talked, wagged like a wizard's finger. We sat down in the shade, cross-legged, as we broke out our lunches. The weather cooperated, sending us an arid sun and a soft wind. He brought out an impressive spread, that to me, hiding a salami and cheese sandwich, looked like a small banquet on the grass. Jars of mayonnaise, mustard, and pickles, a bag of potato chips, and a sack of sandwiches were pulled one by one from a bulging day pack. He then, ceremoniously, put together his meal.

"What I can't stand," he finally said, "is the noise up here
sometimes. I try to get away twice a week from the city and things and come up here for a little relaxation. Then I find some guy with a radio blaring away, drowning out the wind, birds, and everything. Mustard? Chips?"

"No thanks."

"Well, it's downright sacrilegious. I think they ought to ban that stuff or make them keep it nailed to their ear. Even at home the wife keeps the tv at a solid buzz in the background. Pickles?"

"No thanks. I shouldn't. I need to finish my hike this afternoon so I'd better stay with a light lunch."

He crunched into a dill pickle and peered around the bowl of meadows and trees.

He said: "What I can't understand is why anybody would want to change the silence up here. It's damn near perfect."

It *was* damn near perfect—the sky, the sun, the pale gray towers, the rigid trees, the birds—the whole sweet mixture that promotes so much human contentment. We ate our meals, he his generous smorgasbord, and I my spartan brunch. When it was time to leave, I swung my pack over my shoulder and asked him if he'd like to accompany me up the trail.

"No, I don't think so," he replied. "I think I'll just sit here for a while, putter around a bit, and then head back to the car over yonder. Besides, I don't think I could move for a while. Cheesecake before you go?"

"What flavor?"

The Jeep chugged up Trail Ridge Road the next morning, passed by descending and erratic VWs, Scouts, MGs, old Dodge trucks, and slender Porches, their occupant's heads protruding from windows and looking at everything but the road. I survived the long climb to the top. The road snakes along the Continental Divide and reaches at its summit over 12,000 feet.

There was a good stiff wind howling over the surrounding peaks when I pulled into a parking area and put some extra tension on the brake. Standing by the road, I looked out over the alpine backyard and sensed how the Olympian gods felt about the magic of mountains and how such mortal things as washing dishes, mowing lawns, and mailing letters seemed so hopelessly everyday and tied to the life in the foothills below.

As I circled around the tourist cars and moved onto the tundra slopes, I heard snatches of conversation that to the traveler are signals that people are enjoying themselves:

From a boy: "I wonder how far I'd roll if I fell off this ledge."

Or: "Is this higher than the North Pole?"

And: "Who forgot the camera? Jane was that you?"

Or: "Show me where we live again. C'mon, point to Nebraska. Oh, is it *that* far."

And: "Johnny, you're just going to have to wait five minutes till we get in the car and drive to a potty."

Off to the side of the road mosses and lichens smother the bald hills; marmots sunbathe on the large rocks with nothing between them and heaven. Void of the distractions of trees and shadows, the tundra field is a complex design of harshness, tenderness, and pale color.

Down Trail Ridge Road is Estes Park, east of the Continental Divide and one of the civilizing outposts in Colorado of the nineteenth century. In 1873 the tiny colony welcomed journalist Isabella Bird.

She was four feet eleven, English, and as stubborn as the mining camps that she loathed. Flat land bored her, mining towns inspired not a flicker of goodwill in her, but mountains, especially the mountains around Longs Peak, enthralled her. Moreover, she wished to climb one, and like the characters of myth, subdue and arrest some of the power at its summit.

Most Britishers loved Colorado, proclaiming it the Switzerland of America, but Isabella Bird kept an icy distance from most members of the English colony at Estes Park. For one thing Isabella observed that "they neither know how to hold their tongues nor to carry their personal pretensions." She called them "high toners" and preferred the company of the locals, especially a one-eyed, lovable mountain man named Jim Nugent.

In October 1873, Isabella and Jim prepared their ascent of Longs Peak, just south of Estes Park. That morning Isabella dressed in a traditional outfit of bloomers and boots. After riding to the base and hiking a short distance, they camped and spent the night in freezing temperatures at 11,000 feet. The following morning they tramped the 1,000 feet to the beginning of the "serious" climb—the remaining 2,000 feet of sheer pink rock.

Jim looked quite the serious guide in his "high boots, with a
baggy pair of old trousers made of deer hide, held on by an old scarf tucked into them." For Isabella, the following six hours would be fraught with horror, loathing, and one final burst of rapture.

The Climber's Tale

Two thousand feet of solid rock towered above us, four thousand feet of broken rock shelved precipitously below; smooth granite ribs with barely foothold stood out here and there; melted snow refrozen several times, presented a more serious obstacle; many of the rocks were loose and tumbled down when touched. To me it was a time of extreme terror.

I was roped to Jim, but it was of no use; my feet were paralyzed and slipped on the bare rock, and he said it was useless to try to go that way, and we retraced our steps. I wanted to return to the Notch, knowing that my incompetence would detain the party, and one of the young men said almost plainly that a woman was a dangerous encumbrance, but the trapper replied shortly that if it were not to take the lady up he would not go up at all. . . .

After descending about 2,000 feet to avoid the ice we got into a deep ravine with inaccessible sides, partly filled with ice and snow and partly with large and small fragments of rock, which were constantly giving way, rendering the footing very insecure. That part to me was two hours of painful and unwilling submission to the inevitable; of trembling, slipping, straining, of smooth ice appearing when it was least expected, and of weak entreaties to be left behind while the others went on. Jim always said that there was no danger, that there was only a short bad bit ahead, and that I should go up even if he carried me!

Slipping, faltering, gasping from the exhausting toil in the rarefied air, with throbbing hearts and panting lungs, we reached the top of the gorge and squeezed ourselves between two gigantic fragments of rock by a passage called the "Dog's Lift," when I climbed on the shoulders of one man and then was hauled up. This introduced us by an abrupt turn around the southwest angle of the Peak to a narrow shelf of considerable length, rugged, uneven, and so overhung by the cliff in some places that it was necessary to crouch to pass at all.

Above, the Peak looks nearly vertical for 400 feet; then below, the most tremendous precipice I have ever seen descends in one unbroken fall. This is usually considered the most dangerous part of the ascent. . . . There and on the final—and to my thinking the worst—part of the climb, one slip and a breathing, thinking human being would lie 3,000 feet below, a shapeless, bloody heap. . . .

From thence the view is more magnificent even than from the Notch. At the foot of the precipice below us lay a lovely lake, wood embosomed, from or near which St. Vrain and other streams take their rise. . . . Snowy ranges, one behind the other, extended to the distant horizon, folding in their wintry embrace the beauties of Middle Park. Pikes Peak, more than one hundred miles off, lifted that vast but shapeless summit which is the landmark of southern Colorado.

There were snow patches, snow slashes, snow abysses, snow forlorn and soiled looking, snow pure and dazzling, snow glistening above the purple robe of pine worn by all the mountains; while away to the east in the limitless breadth stretched the green-gray of the endless Plains. . . . On the Plains we traced the rivers by their fringe of cottonwoods to the distant Platte, and between us and them lay glories of mountain, canyon and lake sleeping in depths of blue and purple most ravishing to the eye. . . .

Scaling, not climbing, is the correct term for this last ascent. It took one hour to accomplish 500 feet, pausing for breath every minute or two. The only foothold was in narrow cracks or in minute projections on the granite. To get a toe in these cracks, or here and there on a scarcely obvious projection, while crawling on hands and knees, all the while tortured with thirst and gasping and struggling for breath—this was the climb. But at last the Peak was won. A grand well-defined mountian top it is, a nearly level acre of boulders, with precipitous sides all round, the one we came up being the only accessible one.

It was not possible to remain long. One of the young men was seriously alarmed by bleeding from the lungs, and the intense dryness of the day and the rarefication of the air at a height of nearly 15,000 feet made respiration very painful. . . . We all suffered severely from the want of water, and the gasping for breath made our mouths and tongues so dry that articulation was difficult and the speech of all unnatural. . . .

We placed our names, with the date of ascent, in a tin within a crevice and descended to the Ledge, sitting on the smooth granite, getting our feet into cracks and against projections, and letting ourselves down by our hands, Jim going before me so that I might steady my feet against his powerful shoulders. I was no longer giddy and faced the precipice of 3,500 feet without a shiver. . . .

With great difficulty and much assistance I recrossed the Lava Beds, was carried to the horse and lifted upon it, and laid on the ground wrapped up in blankets, a humiliating termination of a great exploit. The horses were saddled and the young men were all ready to start, but Jim quietly said, "Now, gentlemen, I want a good night's rest, and we shan't stir from here tonight." I believe they were really glad to have it so, as one of them was quite finished. I retired to my arbor, wrapped myself in a roll of blankets and was soon asleep.

When I awoke, the moon was high, shining through the silvery branches, whitening the bald peak above the glittering on the great abyss of snow behind, and pine logs were blazing like a bonfire in the cold, still air. My feet were so icy cold that I could not sleep again and getting some blankets to sit in, and making a roll of them for my back, I sat for two hours by the campfire. It was weird and gloriously beautiful. . . . Except for the tones of our voices and an occasional crackle and splutter as a pine knot blazed up, there was no sound on the mountainside. . . .

Once only some wild animals prowled near the camp . . . and the horses, which were picketed by the stream, broke their lariats, stampeded and came rushing wildly towards the fire, and it was fully half an hour before they were caught and quiet restored. Jim—or Mr. Nugent as I always scrupulously called him—told stories of his early youth and of a great sorrow which had led him to embark on a lawless and desperate life. His voice trembled and tears rolled down his cheek. Was it semi-conscious acting, I wondered, or was his dark soul really stirred to its depths by the silence, the beauty and the memories of youth?

We must leave Jim and Isabella and the fire which perhaps provoked too many memories. Actually, Jim's torn emotions healed by morning, and they rode back to Estes Park under a warm October sun. For the rest of the week the English colony heard of the climb and of the perilous exploits of one of the first women on Longs Peak.

I drove down the same main street where Jim and Isabella had cantered home, and where a wall of water in 1982 turned the thoroughfare into a river. Now only a pale watermark remains of that sudden surge of mountain water. Still, there is a persistent resort feeling here, a pleasant vestige of the English colony which flourished under the tutelage of Lord Dunraven.

I turned south at the Big Thompson River, which rages inexorably to the South Platte, and passed Twin Sisters and Isabella Bird's beloved Longs Peak. For a moment I reflected on her ascent of its rock walls and how she met every Everest with customary and English nonchalance, resourcefulness, and pure pluck.

Gravity pulled me into Nederland, a town clinging to the hills around Boulder Creek and described by Helen Hunt Jackson in the 1870s as "a dismal little mining town." It is no longer dismal or very much of a mining town.

By midafternoon I was tempted to seek accommodations. But finding myself on the long end of time and the short end of comfort, I decided on a compromise. I drove into a modest motel and asked the manager for a room. She had the beauty of age and wisdom, and I still remember her taking the key of number six and handing it to me, saying: "The pipes make a little noise, but otherwise the room is spotless." I paid her up front for the room.

I then ran around to the Jeep and packed a few things into the room. I placed a smattering of articles on the bed, plugged in one of those little coffee pots that heat water and instant coffee,

took a fresh, pillowy towel from the rack, and entered the large
shower.

For fifteen solid minutes I scrubbed and washed like a miner, whistled in the steam, sang about the Rockies and anything else that came to mind, wished for nothing. The pipes sang too, but I didn't care.

I toweled myself off and drank a hot cup of the dank liquid from the coffee pot, and dressed in the sunlight filtering through the blinds. Briefly I sighed a long sigh to conclude and summarize such a refreshing interlude. I took one last gulp of coffee, repacked the Jeep, returned the key to the manager's office, admitting to her: "You were right about the pipes, though they're just a little off key." Then I smiled, sensing her surprise, thanked her for the brief stay, and then I steered down the road into a town closer to my destination.

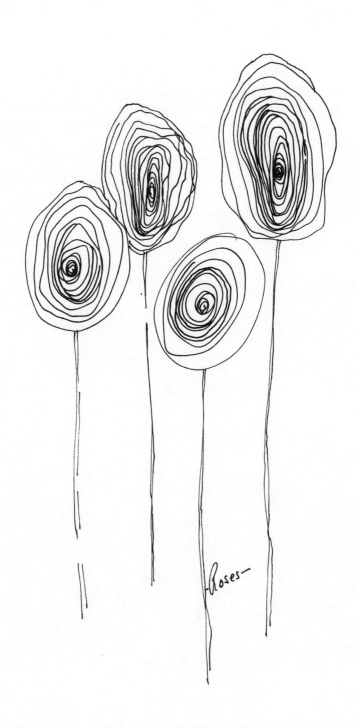

Roses—

14

Central City

October 15:

Just when you think you have seen the last of the mining camps, a little knot of them west of Denver stuns you into sobriety: Black Hawk, Russell Gulch, and Central City. But now the hard and exposed edges have been polished by modern culture, so that these small outposts are much more provocative relics than eyesores. Particularly Central City, known of course for its opera, is so clean and peaceful that it is difficult to conjure up scenes of blowing dust, mule trains, and fires to disrupt the normal ebb and flow of tourists and music lovers.

It was Sunday morning in Central City. A pall of silence hung over the cliff dwellings and the pragmatic brick thoroughfare of Main Street. The wind stirred slightly, but the richest square mile on earth was as shiftless and lifeless as death. The air was dry, tinder dry, as the throat before coffee, and as arid as the hills that all summer long had soaked like sponges the dry suns and winds.

This Golconda cleft from the hills had everything in 1874: saloons, dancehalls, playhouses, banks, and businesses—everything but an adequate water system. Nature gave and nature took away. In an oasis of gold, the skies were as dry as flour.

To Francis Young the problem seemed insoluble. A New Yorker, Young had followed the tide of gold fever from Gotham to Colorado in 1865. By then the news of the wealth of the Colorado mountains had reached Europe, Asia, and around the earth. Young yearned to be "a part of the clan" that stayed on, worked the mines, and wrested from the hills the tons upon tons of gold.

On May 21, 1874, Central City pursued its normal amount of excitement until midmorning, when, as Young explains, nature revolted on Main Street.

The Miner's Tale

It has come at last!

We have been predicting it, discussing it, dreading it—doing everything, in fact, but preparing for it—for lo! these ten years. Today the town has been laid low by fire; and tonight a thousand luckless people—half crazed men, hysterical women and weeping little ones—are camped on the mountainside under the open sky while the stars shine down upon a broad level waste of glowing cinders in the plateau below them where this morning stood their homes. . . .

It has been a notable day in the history of the little town. . . . Although the time measured but a few hours, the various phases of the desperate fight for home and property, and life itself, followed so closely one upon another, in such bewildering detail and in an atmosphere of such mad excitement, as to suffice for the experience of a lifetime. . . .

It was a beautiful morning that ushered in this eventful May day . . . with nothing of portent in the still air to indicate in the slightest degree the frightful nearness of the doom that hung over it. There was only the ever-present danger lurking in the fact that the town was closely built of frame houses and log cabins, bordering on narrow streets, and on which the intense, dry heat of the Colorado sun had beaten steadily for a dozen summers. . . .

By the middle of the morning everything had settled down into the usual humdrum routine of the day: everyone was in his accustomed place, the breadwinner underground, the child in the gray schoolhouse on the hillside, or the merchant in his shop; and except for the continuous passage of the quartz wagons on their way to the mills below, there was nothing in the streets to disturb the tranquility. . . .

Suddenly a cry is heard, and a light wreath of smoke rises in the air over by the foot of Spring Gulch—an obscure corner of town—and two or three frightened Chinamen emerge hurriedly into the little side street at the end of which is the frame shanty they use as a laundry. Their hysterical jabberings direct attention to the building, and quickly a crowd is drawn to the scene. A few cool-headed men realize that a fire has started in this nest of dry frames, and without delay the fire bell is rung, the precious buckets are handed out, and a line of willing hands quickly formed to the gulch, glad of so early an opportunity for a practical demonstration of the discipline of the last few months. . . .

But now the time for action has come, in one dread moment is revealed the terrible truth which none has dreamed of—the one emergency overlooked in the weighty deliberations of the fathers of the commune—the gulch is dry!

The flames have burst out of the roof of the Chinese shack, and guided by the light prevailing current, have already leaped over and licked up the roofs of two or three adjoining shanties before the crowd had thrown off its stupor and begun to cast about for other means of staying their further progress toward Main Street—a course which they seem to be following as accurately as though drawn thither by a magnet.

Axes are procured and gallant and perilous work is done squarely in the teeth of the advancing fire, in the attempt to make a gap in its road by demolishing two or three frames just ahead of it; but the fighters have barely time to jump for their lives before the flames, which have gathered strength and intensity in every foot of their progress, leap over the space and attack with fury the last little row of frames that stand between them and the town's principal thoroughfare . . . and all this is the work of a short quarter of an hour.

Now a general alarm is sounded, and it's "fall in everybody" to save the town. But indeed there is no need of general alarm: the fire has been its own advance courier, and the whole town is now aroused and, conscious of its own danger, is already crowding into the streets. . . .

With one wild leap the fire crosses Main Street and turning to the right marches on a resistless way in two parallel lines down toward the town's center. The street is long—it is the main artery of the town. At its lower end it intersects at right angles another business thoroughfare, hardly second in importance. Toward the head of this, and but fifty yards above the intersection, facing each other on opposite sides of the street, are the town's largest two buildings, the Teller House and the Masonic Temple; and these are such solid structures of brick and stone as to afford a good fighting chance of stopping the flames at this point and saving the residence section.

Some old wells have been uncovered close by in the frantic hunt for water, and a water reserve has been found in the hotel itself, together with a hose, ladders and other paraphernalia, and all these may be used to good purpose if effort is organized and concentrated here. The decision is quickly made and it is so ordered.

A backward glance up Main Street discovers the utter hopelessness of wasting labor there. . . . The flames are leaping in forked tongues fifty feet across the roadway or from one roof to another. . . . The street must go. . . . It is a hard message to the dazed merchants, standing guard over the piles of goods at their doorways. . . . With the recklessness of despair they tacitly surrender. The scene has already become one of awful grandeur, and they stand fascinated at the fierce approach of the flames toward them; indeed, some laugh in a wild sort of way when at last the van of the fiery column begins its attack on the particular tenement which encloses all their worldly possessions. . . .

Here they camp under the open sky, the women and children in shrinking groups gathering their household goods about them; the erstwhile male hermits of no family attachments light their pipes and sullenly look down upon the scene, helplessly inactive, for there is nothing else for them to do. Presently their numbers are increased by the stricken merchants, their arms laden with incongruous bits of salvage pulled from the shelves or from the street piles at the last moment without regard to value. . . fully a thousand homeless people, ranged in lines, terrace-like, one above the other on the face of the mountain which overlooks Central City. . . .

Meantime reinforcements in generous numbers are coming in from immediately roundabout; and the telegraph has spread the news abroad, so that by noon from as far away as Golden fire engines and men are arriving by special trains. . . . A determined stand is made at the Teller House, which is successful after a stubborn fight of two or three hours. Down the long reach of the same street, however, the fire is of necessity allowed to work its own sweet will on the closely built frame and log structures on either side . . . until the whole is leveled with the ground, save two or three isolated bricks which have miraculously survived the ordeal. . . . And all this has occupied but a half-dozen hours of a summer day. . . .

In late afternoon, when some measure of order is restored and the fire at last under control, the Teller House becomes the natural rendezvous of the burnt-out citizens and the exhausted firefighters, and by and by it is overrun with a stranger gathering than ever did or ever will again come together within its walls. Whatever may have been the social differences in the town yesterday are for the time forgotten, both here and on the streets. . . . Barriers were indeed burned away in the great catastrophe, and now the general welfare is the one common concern of all. It is a still excited and reckless—but withal a jovial and sympathetic—crowd, exchanging experiences and congratulations, fighting the day's battles o'er again, counting heads, computing losses, and thanking God that it is no worse.

October 16:

From Central City the road spirals south into the dirt heaved into mountains around Idaho Springs. From there west the highway soars gradually, following Clear Creek, and shoots through the enormous cleavage in the Front Range.

All along, from Cripple Creek and Victor to Ouray and now Central City I had been forced to deal with effects of mining. Some towns effectively disguise their mines; some bear no traces of them at all; still others expose their miserable effects like proud and contemptible landlords. I have also seen the

Rhondda Valley in Wales and parts of Nottingham in England. Talk of your mines and the refrigeration of the spirit. Parts of Wales are so rich in coal that the natural tendency is to leave neither soil, sod, nor tree. The black hills stretch endlessly unbroken by the slightest shade of green or vertical twig.

Just down the road is Georgetown, a hodgepodge of domestic architectural styles all squeezed into one of the most charming square miles in Colorado. Here is Georgian next to Cape Cod, baroque next to gingerbread. And somehow it works.

By noon I had swung the Jeep off the highway and pulled into one of the many tiny restaurants that crowd the center of town. Over a steaming bowl of vegetable soup I asked the waitress if she knew anything of the Hotel de Paris across the street.

"I don't, but Eddie probably does."

"Eddie?"

"Eddie's the cook. He should be over the noon rush about one thirty. Why don't you come back and ask for him then."

I did. I was shown into the large kitchen, filled now with dirty dishes, brass tubs, and steam. Over in the corner at a table sat Eddie. He was fifty, I guessed, a bit overweight and smoked a prodigious cigar. I asked him about the hotel. But he told me about Louis Du Puy.

"Louis du Puy *was* the Hotel de Paris. Gerard was his real name. He was born in France and came into quite an inheritance. But he blew that quickly. Then he served in the French army, deserted, and headed for London and New York. Nothing worked for him. Around 1870, I think, he came West and settled in Georgetown. About that time, war broke out in Europe and he thought of returning to fight."

"The Franco-Prussian War."

"Huh?"

"Never mind," I said, "Go on."

"Well, he stayed here and worked the mines. Then about five years later an explosion in a mine nearly killed him. The people here took up a collection for Louis to set him up in a business. Well, he bought the bakery building and furnished it with French furniture and paintings and mirrors. Real classy stuff—and that was the birth of the Hotel de Paris. From then on it was the most famous hotel in the West."

"And Louis, who *was* he?"

"Ah, Louis was a strange one, a real strange one. He hated women. Why I don't know. But he wouldn't let a woman near the hotel unless he approved of her beforehand. When he died he left the hotel to a woman named Sophie. Then she died shortly thereafter. Louis didn't make sense, do you know what I mean?"

I nodded.

"He didn't particularly like his guests, either. If he didn't like you he'd ask you to get off the premises. It became a real honor to get to your room unchallenged, I suppose. People even wagered outside whether or not they could get by the fearsome Louis du Puy."

"And he was serious?"

"Very much so. That was his castle, and he was the king who wanted to know how his subjects were behaving. If he didn't like them, they left—period. Once he fought a bunch of tax collectors who demanded the hotel be taxed. He raised a shotgun at them and even threatened to burn the hotel with himself inside."

. I thanked Eddie and crossed the street to the Hotel de Paris. In the warm afternoon light, you can still see the parted curtain on the second floor, and the eyes of Louis du Puy scrupulously inspecting his empire on the street below.

15

Mountain and Plain

The real lovers of Colorado, those who trudged from the restrictive society of the East and fell under the spell of these mountains—Bierstadt, Moran, Young, and Bird—seem like adolescent admirers compared with the high priest of the viscera, Walt Whitman.

There is little doubt that Whitman fell desperately in love with these hills in 1879. A lifelong traveler, Whitman usually wintered in Camden, New Jersey, and spent his summers in Missouri, Canada, Long Island, and Kansas. In early September of 1879, he began the long overland rail journey which eventually deposited him in this high and wide valley of South Park.

Before the Eisenhower Tunnel was erected, this was the chief passage to the Continental Divide from Denver—down from Kenosha Pass and up to the mining camps of Breckenridge and Leadville. Now, this vast Mojave with grass dips unevenly to reveal the raised serrated edge of the Continental Divide and forms one of those long stretches, exhausting to the eye as it is to the heart.

But it was this high plateau of South Park, bowing down to let the far mountains appear more dramatic, that first hypnotized a wide-eyed Whitman. By anyone's standards, Whitman was a latecomer to the West. In the year (1863) that Bierstadt was puttering around Colorado in tweeds, Whitman was toiling as a wound-dresser in Washington. He had already made his reputation with *Leaves of Grass*, but spent much of the Civil War close to hospital beds caring for the legions of sick and dying men. He never recovered from its miseries or the memories of its horrors. It was "the great wild buffalo," as he proclaimed himself, who in *Leaves of Grass* had exalted the Westward movement:

Colorado men are we,
From the peaks gigantic, from the great sierras/
and the high plateaus,
From the mine and from the gully, from the hunting trail/
we come,
Pioneers! O Pioneers!

Fighting bouts of ill-health throughout his fifties, Whitman traveled West for the first time at age sixty (1879) and temporarily found his stamina and rediscovered the pioneering spirit that he had trumpeted from the New York sidewalks. He stayed in Denver and enjoyed side trips, as Bierstadt had done, in the mountains above it. One memorable journey west of the city prompted Whitman's pen to race over the paper—jottings, notations, and scribbles that reveal the deep affect of color, light, and landforms. He plunged into the trip's pace with characteristic energy, distracted by the sights more like a child in Wonderland than a man growing gray. (*Specimen Days*).

The Poet's Tale

AN HOUR ON KENOSHA SUMMIT

Jottings from the Rocky Mountains, mostly pencill'd during a day's trip over the South Park RR., returning from Leadville, and especially the hour we were detain'd, (much to my satisfaction,) at Kenosha summit. As afternoon advances, novelties, far-reaching splendors, accumulate under the bright sun in the pure air. But I had better commence with the day.

The confronting of Platte cañon just at dawn, after a ten miles' ride in early darkness on the rail from Denver—the

seasonable stoppage at the entrance of the cañon, and good
breakfast of eggs and trout and nice griddle cakes—then as we
travel on, and get well in the forge, all the wonders, beauty,
savage power of the scene—the wild stream of water, from
sources of snows, brawling continually in sight one side—the
dazzling sun, and the morning lights on the rocks—such turns
and grades in the track, squirming around corners, or up and
down hills—far glimpses of a hundred peaks, titanic neck-
laces, stretching north and south—the huge rightly-named
Dome rock—and as we dash along, others similar, simple,
monolithic, elephantine.

AN EGOTISTICAL "FIND"

"I have found the law of my own poems," was the unspoken
but more-and-more decided feeling that came to me as I
pass'd, hour after hour, amid all this grim yet joyous elemental
abandon—this plenitude of material, entire absence of art, un-
trammel'd play of primitive Nature—the chasm, the gorge, the
crystal mountain stream, repeated scores, hundreds of miles—
the broad handling and absolute uncrampedness—the fantas-
tic forms, bathe in transparent browns, faint reds and grays,
towering sometimes a thousand, sometimes two or three
thousand feet high—at their tops now and then huge masses
pois'd, and mixing with the clouds, with only their outlines,
hazed in misty lilac, visible. . . .

ART FEATURES

Talk, I say again, of going to Europe, of visiting the ruins of
feudal castles, or Coliseum remains, or kings' palaces—when
you can come *here*. The alternations one gets, too; after the Il-
linois and Kansas prairies of a thousand miles—smooth and
easy areas of the corn and wheat of ten million democratic
farms in the future—here start up in every conceivable presentation of shape, these non-utilitarian piles, coping the skies,
emanating a beauty, terror, power, more than Dante or Angelo
ever knew. Yes, I think the chyle of not only poetry and painting, but oratory, and even the metaphysics and music fit for
the New World, before being finally assimilated, need first and
feeding visits here.

Mountain streams.—The spiritual contrast and etheriality of the whole region consist largely to me in its never-absent peculiar streams—the snows of inaccessible upper areas melting and running down through the gorges continually. Nothing like the water of the pastoral plains, or creeks with wooded banks and turf, or anything of the kind elsewhere. The shapes that element takes in the shows of the globe cannot be fully understood by an artist until he has studied these unique rivulets.

Aerial effects.—But perhaps as I gaze around me the rarest sight of all is in atmospheric hues. The prairies—as I cross'd them in my journey hither—and these mountains and parks, seem to me to afford new lights and shades. Everywhere the aerial gradations and sky-effects inimitable; nowwhere else such perspectives, such transparent lilacs and grays. I can conceive of some superior landscape painter, some fine colorist, after sketching awhile out here, discarding all his previous work, delightful to stock exhibition amateurs, as muddy, raw and artificial. Near one's eye ranges an infinite variety; high up, the bare whitey-brown, above timber line; in certain spots afar patches of snow any time of year; (no trees, no flowers, no birds, at those chilling altitudes). As I write I see the Snowy Range through the blue mist, beautiful and far off. I plainly see the patches of snow.

DENVER IMPRESSIONS

Through the long-lingering half-light of the most superb of evenings we return'd to Denver, where I staid several days leisurely exploring, receiving impressions, with which I may as well taper off this memorandum, itemizing what I say there. The best was the men, three-fourths of them large, able, calm, alert, American. And cash! why they create it here. Out in the smelting works, (the biggest and most improv'd ones, for the precious metals, in the world,) I saw long rows of vats, pans, cover'd by bubbling-boiling water, and fill'd with pure silver, four or five inches thick, many thousand dollars' worth in a pan. The foreman who was showing me shovel'd it carelessly up with a little wooden shovel, as one might toss beans. Then large silver bricks, worth $2000 a brick, dozens of piles, twenty

in a pile. In one place in the mountains, at a mining camp, I
had a few days before seen rough bullion on the ground in
the open air, like the confectioner's pyramids at some swell
dinner in New York. . . .

A city, this Denver, well-laid out—Laramie street, and 15th
and 16th and Champa streets, with others, particularly fine—
some with tall storehouses of stone and iron, and windows of
plate-glass—all the streets with little canals of mountain water
running along the sides—plenty of people, "business,"
moderness—yet not without a certain racy wild smack, all its
own. A place of fast horses, (many mares with their colts,) and
I saw lots of big greyhounds for antelope hunting. Now and
then groups of miners, some just come in, some starting out,
very picturesque.

One of the papers here interview'd me, and reported me as
saying off-hand: "I have lived in or visited all the great cities
on the Atlantic third of the republic—Boston, Brooklyn with
its hills, New Orleans, Baltimore, stately Washington, broad
Philadelphia, teeming Cincinnati and Chicago, and for thirty
years in that wonder, wash'd by hurried and glittering tides,
my own New York, not only the New World's but the world's
city—but, newcomer to Denver as I am, and threading its
streets, breathing its air, warm'd by its sunshine and having
what there is of its human as well as aerial ozone flash'd upon
me now for only three or four days, I am very much like a
man feels sometimes toward certain people he meets with,
and warms to, and hardly knows why. I, too, can hardly tell
why, but as I enter'd the city in the slight haze of a late September afternoon, and have breath'd its air, and slept well
o'nights, and have roam'd or rode leisurely, and watch'd the
comers and goers at the hotels, and absorb'd the climatic
magnetism of this curiously attractive region, there has steadily grown upon me a feeling of affection for the spot, which,
sudden as it is, has become so definite and strong that I must
put it on record."

So much for my feeling toward the Queen city of the plains
and peaks, where she sits in her delicious rare atmosphere,
over 5000 feet above sea-level, irrigated by mountain streams,
one way looking east over the prairies for a thousand miles,

and having the other, westward, in constant view by day, draped in their violet haze, mountain tops innumerable. Yes, I fell in love with Denver, and even felt a wish to spend my declining and dying days there.

And why didn't he? Whitman never mentioned what prompted his return journey, or what urged him onto the eight o'clock train the next morning. I suspect that he needed the coterie of friends in New Jersey and New York, the comfortable digs in Camden, and the insular society and rules of the East, in spite of all the "rarefied air" and "democratic vistas" that abounded in Colorado.

But such praise for a city! Looking out over Denver, the mountains struggling for air, the glass cages piercing a layer of pollution as ugly as coal dust, I found it tough to share Whitman's enthusiasm for the air or the ground.

But when the wind does shove the dirt southward, the city is reborn, and becomes the Queen City of the Plains once again. Louis Vasquez's trading post of 1832 mushroomed around the South Platte River, gained impetus in the 1850s with injections of Kansas refugees, and by 1859, twenty years before Whitman's arrival, Denver had become a patchwork of cabins, saloons, and mercantiles clustered around the river. The city matured, hemmed in by the Arapaho and Cheyenne who controlled the lands ringing the city.

Then words of gold were on people's lips. Cherry Creek. Gregory Gulch. Buckskin Joe. Golden. Towns were thrown together as quickly as miners cashed in their nuggets. The alarm went out, mostly by word of mouth, producing the influx of men, boys, itinerants, and speculators, whose movements and antics had so captivated Whitman in 1879.

If the great poet was dazed by this feverish activity, an earlier traveler, Horace Greeley (editor of the New York *Tribune*), was critical of Denver's "vigorous" lifestyle, finding "more brawls, more fights, more pistol shots with criminal intent in this log city of one hundred and fifty dwellings, not three-fourths completed nor two-thirds inhabited, nor one-third fit to be, than in any community of no greater numbers on earth." During his trip in 1859, Greeley was further intrigued by how cabins were acquired in midcity. If you were attracted by an uninhabited cabin,

you entered it, threw your gear on the floor, spread out your
blankets, and ate your bacon and beans under its feeble roof.
"Jumping cabins" became a popular means of survival. Greeley
fell victim to the practice and even found himself enjoying a
miner's simple lifestyle in the rustic, if porous, accommodations.

A magpie soaring above modern Denver could unmistakably
see how Horace Greeley's matchstick cabins had been replaced
by an eruption of skyscrapers downtown and close to a winding
loop of the South Platte. Flying north and east the magpie would
notice more substantial flying machines at Stapleton Airport, and
then turning north, gathering speed, he could swoop down over
the grim rectangle of Rocky Mountain Arsenal, and then dip and
dive over the alfalfa fields due north. Banking, turning south, he
could see the mountains, shadowed and snow-smeared, coming
into view on his right, and he could pick out new suburbs breaking brightly through old ones. The wind would carry him now,
bear him back over the severe grid of the city, and he would
notice a concentration of north-south, east-west intersections,
except at a convergence of the South Platte and Cherry Creek
where they were splintered by diagonals. Finally, sensing that he
was capable of one last great gesture, he would spiral downward
in long, lingering flight and spread his wings over the city, over
the high, clean buildings standing on old shoulders, and glide
serenely over the city that was not on the eve of its destiny, but
already beginning to experience it.

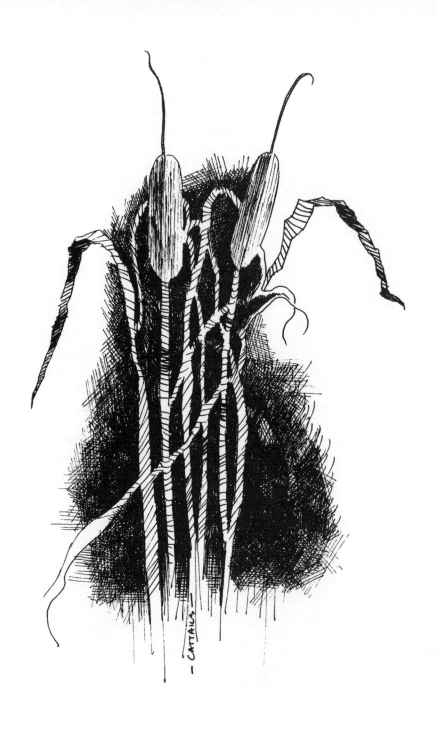

16

Wisdom of the Hills

"Spirit that Form'd This Scene"
Written in Platte Cañon, Colorado

Spirit that form'd this scene,
These tumbled rock-piles grim and red,
These reckless heaven-ambitious peaks,
These gorges, turbulent-clear streams, this naked freshness,
These formless wild arrays, for reasons of their own;
I know thee, savage spirit—we have communed together,
Mine too such wild arrays, for reasons of their own;
Was't charged against my chants they had forgotten art?
To fuse within themselves its rules precise and delicatesse?
The lyrist's measur'd beat, the wrought-out temple's
grace—column and polish'd arch forgot?
But thou that revelest here—spirit that form'd this scene,
They have remember'd thee.

Platte Canyon, October 18:

Not much has changed since Whitman wrote those words in this canyon just below Kenosha Pass. The trees and shrubs have spread considerably, but the restless, heaven-bound rocks still soar like angry fingers, weathered and bleached.

I had just come from Breckenridge and Fairplay and steered this way into the monumental silence of the pass. South Park snakes to the horizon under a brass sun and an empty sky.

So with Whitman I have come home, not to the cities where I began but to these eternal hills that possess the secrets and hold the wealth of our state: a place as rich in nature as it is in metals.

We stand at a time far different than the tenderfoot innocence of Whitman's. In 1880 Denver stretched out on the plains, aspired toward an easy heaven, swaggered to the hills with its gold and silver, and was guided into the promising future by natives and streams of migrants from the East. One could say, as Whitman did, that a sense of plenitude descended on the city and became apparent in the way it pursued its independence and indifference.

But we haved killed the buffalo, torn the hills in Central City and Cripple Creek, polluted the skies, and dismembered the landscape. Do we dare enter the new age with the old weapons?

Why have I come to Shawnee, Colorado? There are no hotels, swimming pools, groomed slopes, or ski schools, only a half dozen or so modest cottages sprinkled on the hills. I had come for a rendezvous, and the weather, the hills, and the dry road that winds down from Kenosha Pass had obliged.

I turned into a driveway that sloped considerably upward, so that I had to proceed in first gear. Just below, the South Platte gathers force and turns into the raging stream that eventually splits Denver into two halves.

After proceeding about thirty feet up the drive, it snaked, and brought me to a level spot with this sign staked by the side:

GO BACK!
No Solicitors
Animals Welcome

My first thought was to submit, but there must be in everybody some temptation to avoid obeying certain signs, traffic or otherwise. Besides, I was not ready to be intimidated.

I took the long winding driveway in about three minutes, arriving at the white cottage at its head. I could not say whether it was the warmth of the day, the serenity of the hills, the murmur of the forest, or even the face of the man approaching me—but as I stopped in the dust something was signaling the resolution and completion of my search. I had known moments on my journey, brief sunlit moments—in Victor, Beaver Creek, Mesa Verde, Maroon Bells, Vail, Rocky Mountain National Park— epiphanies that illuminated and enclosed both me and my sur- roundings. But this moment was different. There was an inside warmth, a clarity of purpose, a sureness of being and a rightness of place.

I held out my hand to the man who limped out of the door and down the steps. There are faces that reflect their place, and his looked like it had been freshly plucked from the soil: strong, lean, and Slavic. I made a joke about the sign in the driveway, we laughed, and went inside.

The day progressed and the afternoon began with one pencil of sunlight falling across soft chairs, and behind us the theater of mountains loomed, made even more indolent by the palest of hazes dropped over them. There are people who tell you every- thing without being provoked by a question. They simply ex- pose their whole lives to you as if they are reading a grocery list or reciting verse or talking about what they did that day. Such was my host. He gestured when he spoke, grew passionate, and the words flowed from his lips as if from a bottomless well. And all I did was listen:

"I came West in 1919 and settled down in Victor. That was just at the end of the glorious days when people staked everything on a big move. I guess we still do, but not like then. There wasn't an adequate system of roads, so often you'd just drive right across someone's land and hope there weren't any rivers ahead.

"I worked as a mucker in the mines for a while. I spent a good deal of my life a thousand feet below the earth. I got to know it quite well down there. Then I left one day and kicked around Colorado and Utah and Arizona.

"From that point on, my view of life changed. I needed a place to stay for the rest of my life. People use the word love a lot— often when they don't mean it—but I genuinely love these forests of the Rockies. I think one thing is certain: anyone must find *that* place, any place. It could be five inches square, or a beach, or a rain forest. No matter. The important thing is that you find it. If you can't live on it, vacation on it. Seek it out. And by associating with it, by breathing its air, it will fill up a necessary part of you. It will crowd out all the ugliness and depravity in the world. It's a place that you know when you find it, that you agree with, and that is worth all the dead ends, wrong turns, and endless trips it takes to find it. But it is that place, or those places, which mean the most and make you what you are."

I know that as I turned down the driveway, snapshots of Longs Peak, forests in Vail, and sandcastles in Mesa Verde flashed through my mind, as well as memories and faces perhaps coaxed to the surface by them. So that was it. I had already found the place I was seeking, already known and breathed its air and felt its suns, already passed through it and knew and it had taken up residence in me.

I could have been running, so quickly the forest fled around me, and interspersed with leaves and light was a film of faces, images, with jumbled dialogues spliced in—Grace McCory, Charlie, Whitman, my heaven-bound walker, Moran, Larry Darnell, the Pueblo artist, Mark—and so many more that fell down and rumbled in the heart. I kept the Jeep going, losing altitude, followed by streams and chased by dissolving light. I would turn south and head home. I would turn on a new forest corner, but I would know that the spiritual journey never ended. The spirit was always moving, doubting, pioneering, resisting, returning and going again. And filling it up and giving it energy were those acres and inches of real estate that we live on, vacation on, travel on, reflect and muse on; their names cling to our minds and their forests and hills give us meaning and sustenance.

So now we stand, new pioneers with new hands and faces, like young Pueblos staring over the arid tables and high mountains of Colorado, searching: broadcaster and baker, rancher and journalist, engineer and artist, doctor and miner, farmer and retailer, businessman and intinerant, emerging into the future and retracing the past, exploring and retreating, creating and preserving, moving as one onto a new promontory, hearing a distant bell,

tolling, tolling, sending us to know and know forever the wisdom of the hills and to know that in coming home is the beginning of our departure.

Vale pilgrim!

The End